REDISCOVER THE JOY
NATURE WITH TO

THE TRACKER
Tom Brown's classic true story—the most powerful and magical high-spiritual adventure since *The Teachings of Don Juan*

THE SEARCH
The continuing story of *The Tracker*, exploring the ancient art of the new survival

THE VISION
Tom Brown's profound personal journey into the ancient mystical experience of vision quests

THE QUEST
The acclaimed outdoorsman shows how we can save our planet

THE JOURNEY
A message of hope and harmony for our Earth and our spirits—Tom Brown's vision for healing our world

GRANDFATHER
The incredible true story of a remarkable Native American and his lifelong search for peace and truth in nature

AWAKENING SPIRITS
For the first time, Tom Brown shares the unique meditation exercises used by students of his personal Tracker classes

THE WAY OF THE SCOUT

Tom Brown's real-life apprenticeship in the ways of the scouts—ancient teachings as timeless as nature itself

THE SCIENCE AND ART OF TRACKING

Tom Brown shares the wisdom of generations of animal trackers—revelations that awaken us to our own place in nature and in the world

AND THE BESTSELLING SERIES OF
TOM BROWN'S FIELD GUIDES

TOM BROWN'S
guide to
HEALING
the EARTH

Tom Brown, Jr., with Randy Walker, Jr.

BERKLEY

NEW YORK

BERKLEY
An imprint of Penguin Random House LLC
penguinrandomhouse.com

"Path of the Earth Steward" copyright © by Philip Martin, PhD

Library of Congress Cataloging-in-Publication Data

Names: Brown, Tom, 1950– author. | Berkley Books.
Title: Tom Brown's guide to healing the earth / Tom Brown, Jr., with Randy Walker, Jr.
Other titles: Guide to healing the earth | Guide to healing the earth.
Description: First Edition. | New York: Berkley, 2019.
Identifiers: LCCN 2019030411 (print)| LCCN 2019030412 (ebook) |
ISBN 9780425257388 (paperback) | ISBN 9780440001218 (eBook)
Subjects: LCSH: Outdoor life. | Environmental responsibility. | Nature conservation.
Classification: LCC GV191.6 | DDC 796.5—dc23
LC record available at https://lccn.loc.gov/2019030412

First Edition: November 2019

Printed in the United States of America
1 3 5 7 9 10 8 6 4 2

Cover art: *Mountains* by Lillian Polley / Arcangel Images
Cover design by Emily Osborne
Book design by Alison Cnockaert
Title page art: *Mountain landscape* by Bioraven / Shutterstock

Most Berkley books are available at special quantity discounts for bulk purchases for sales
promotions, premiums, fund-raising, or educational use. Special books, or book excerpts, can also
be created to fit specific needs. For details, write: SpecialMarkets@penguinrandomhouse.com.

ACKNOWLEDGMENTS

———

I would first like to thank Tom for giving me this opportunity to help him convey in this book Grandfather's vision of caring for and healing the Earth. I would also like to thank Berkley editors Tom Colgan and Grace House for their patience, concise attention to detail and pointing out my mistakes. I appreciate all they have done on this project. My special thanks to Rachael Pecore-Valdez and Rien de Rooij for the comments and corrections they provided on the manuscript. The three of us have been a team ever since we first met in a philosophy class over fifteen years ago, but I never expected them to step up like they have in their help with this book. My gratitude and thanks also go out to all my sister and bother Trackers around the world who carry Grandfather's vision in their hearts.

CONTENTS

FOREWORD

Guide to Healing the Earth is about Grandfather's vision that each (individual) person who chooses to do so can become an effective agent of change in restoring balance in natural environments disrupted and stressed by modern society. To Grandfather's way of thinking, each act of caretaking, no matter how small, makes a difference. The positive energy of each and every act of a caretaker is felt by the natural world. Each positive act sends a form of healing energy to the (Earth and) environment around you in ever-widening circles. It is too overwhelming to try to address all the ways humankind is destroying and polluting our planet. The primary focus of this book is about what one person can do. I've presented numerous ways of how to be a caretaker in this book so one can learn ways to interact with the natural world in a healing manner and create areas of balance through action.

This book is to encourage each person who reads it to embrace the fact they can make a difference. You become part of the solution when embracing the role of a caretaker and healer of our Earth Mother. Grandfather led me to understand that nothing can move in nature without affecting everything else around any action, be it a crow's alarm call or the step of a fox in the brush.

Grandfather's vision of leading people back to the Earth was a fundamental part of his life. Throughout his sixty years of wandering throughout North and South America and during the years I was fortunate enough to spend with him, he was constantly exploring new ways to interact with his environment, constantly experiencing awe at the simplest acts in nature. Grandfather would sit with a blueberry bush for hours, watching a single flower as it opened and bloomed. He would place a single grain of sand on the tip of his finger and hold it in the sunlight, marveling for hours at the different patterns that the sunlight revealed as it moved across the sky. This book is my attempt to convey Grandfather's philosophy of life and state of consciousness when acting as a caretaker and healer of the Earth. Throughout the book I'll include some of my stories, experiences and specific examples of Grandfather's ways of caring for what he referred to as our Earth Mother.

Grandfather, through his actions, taught me about approaching the natural world from the perspective of a caretaker. He continually encouraged Rick and me to expand our awareness in every environment. Grandfather taught us to see, on the one hand, the big picture and, on the other hand, the tiniest details of each ecosystem we encountered.

The more Grandfather revealed to me about the part of his vision to heal and honor our Earth Mother, the more I grew to embrace his vision as a part of my own. I have spent the past forty years teaching and sharing Grandfather's philosophies through my books, physical classes at the Tracker School and online classes reaching students around the globe. Grandfather was a coyote teacher, which meant that I had to figure out things through experience. He never revealed every part of a skill or teaching. Only by gaining experience through practicing a particular skill many times did we discover the secrets kept hidden by Grandfather. He knew that discovering something on your own was the best teacher. Grandfather often said there is no such thing as failure, provided that you learn from it. If a skill came easily to me, I would still ask myself what I was missing, feeling that there had to be some aspect of the skill I was failing to see because I often learned more from my failures than from my successes. Sometimes I wanted to experience failure so I could then face the challenge of getting it right.

To Grandfather's people, the Southern Lipan Apache, the coyote was not seen as a symbol of a trickster, as numerous other southwestern Indian tribes did; rather, they viewed the coyote as a revered teacher that held the secrets and wisdom of living with the Earth. The coyote is able to adapt to almost any situation and environment. Coyotes are solitary animals at times, joining together in packs when a group of them is needed to maintain their survival. The coyotes' adaptability enables them to adjust to the carrying capacity of each environment they move through. Their adaptability is a trait that has led to a dramatic increase in their numbers even as man and his machines have constantly shrunk their hunting grounds over the past few hundred years. Coyotes have grown so populous that they now inhabit most of North America. Even Charles Darwin said that it wasn't the strongest of a species that survived or the most intelligent. It was the members of the species that best adapted to changing environments, that were the best propagators of the species. The coyote is a prime example of just that.

Grandfather was not an easy teacher to have from his students' perspective. He seldom smiled or praised our results when working a skill. A neutral grunt from him upon examining a tool or craft that Rick or I was working on or had produced translated into high praise.

He strived to keep us on our guard and to push our skills beyond competency, to the point of complete mastery. If I produced a poorly flaked arrowhead, the look of scorn and disgust Grandfather would give me would first leave me with a feeling of shame that I had let him down. Then his look would spur me on to do a proper job the next time. With Grandfather, you had to be passionate about working on each skill.

Grandfather also made us learn to be proficient with either hand in working a skill, sometimes blindfolded as well. We learned to do the bow drill left- and right-handed. We had to be able to carve wood or flake arrowheads or stone tools with either hand. He said if one side becomes injured, the other side must be competent in the skill. This was in case we should find ourselves injured during a full-survival situation.

As a coyote teacher, Grandfather did not spell things out like our teachers in school. Skills were broken down into sections, which we learned through practice. As our experience grew, we became competent in each stage of the process. Grandfather would direct us to observe a particular animal, when he was teaching a fundamental truth about an aspect of the natural world. For weeks we would track an animal, learn its habits and observe it in nature. Only then, once we knew the animal, would Grandfather continue to reveal more of the lesson he had planned for us to learn.

To Grandfather's people, the coyote was the keeper of the knowledge, a keeper of the wisdom. The coyote were the old man, the old woman of the wilderness. The Lipan held the coyote in the same regard as the Lakota held the spotted eagle, with a similar kind of reverence.

During my nearly eleven years with Grandfather, the coyote teaching never stopped. It started from day one and continued right to the very end of our time together. Grandfather left me with so many things, so many teachings that were open-ended and still, to this day, I have this laundry list of things I continue to experiment with.

Grandfather would say something like "Well, you can make this kind of water basket if you . . ." And then he'd let it go and wouldn't show me the weave or anything else. That kind of subtle motivation was one of those things where you experiment working a skill until you get it right. It's amazing how Grandfather had a way of keeping us not only passionate, but bordering on being obsessive in our efforts. Coyote teachers demand such passion. They won't tolerate laziness.

One of the finest examples of coyote teaching Grandfather gave Rick and me was when we walked into his Primitive Camp deep in the Pine Barrens for the first time. There sat a man with a debris hut, a hide on a rack, a drum, pottery and baskets arranged around his work fire; he was wearing beautiful buckskin clothing. His work area was a collection of skills in process, arranged along with his beautifully crafted primitive tools. His was an exquisite encampment, with a feeling of peace and joy surrounding the entire area. It was the pinnacle of everything I'd always wanted to know and learn.

One of the first sentences out of Grandfather's mouth to Rick and me was "I go home to my people in two weeks." Literally, Grandfather kept this myth going for the next ten-plus years. Out of the blue, Grandfather would tell us he was planning to go back to his people in two weeks, causing Rick and me to redouble our efforts to learn what we could before he left. Grandfather never intended to leave until his job, as he saw it, was done. It was like that with every skill. Of course, every skill came with its mythology, parables of where it had come from, songs that were sung while working it and stories that related to it.

Grandfather had come to the Pine Barrens following his compelling feeling stemming from his vision of a white coyote, which he had received during one of his early vision quests. Grandfather's grand vision led to his decades of wanderings. He had felt compelled to travel thousands of miles to visit his great-grandson, Rick, and to follow where his Inner Vision was leading him.

Rick and I had only just met Grandfather, and now he was telling the two of us that he was leaving in two weeks to go back to his people! If you were in my shoes, what would you do? For me, the answer was simple: I'd do everything I could to learn from him and absorb every tiny detail of knowledge he was willing to share with us during those two weeks.

Perhaps the worst thing students can possibly do is ask a coyote teacher a question about something that they had not researched in depth on their own first, to not take the time to research, when in-depth research would have led them to the answer. I learned this lesson the hard way, much to my shame and humiliation.

One weekend, we were working in camp on a project that demanded that we focus intensely on the intricate weaving of a basket. All during that weekend, I kept hearing this bird down at the lower swamp singing away. I couldn't remember ever hearing that particular bird around camp before. For some reason, the songs of the bird sounded vaguely familiar, but the memory of that birdsong remained just out of reach.

On Sunday, as Rick and I prepared to head back home, I asked, "Grandfather, have you heard that bird singing that different kind of song down in the lower swamp all weekend?" He answered, "Yes, Grandson." I then asked him if he knew what kind of bird it was.

Grandfather looked hard at me, his expression changing to utter disgust. After a painfully long pause, he said, "Grandson, what you have just told me is that you are too lazy to find out for yourself what kind of bird that is. I think I go now to my people."

With that, while Rick and I pleaded with him to stay, Grandfather went up to his shelter, packed his buckskin bags and was quickly on his way out of camp. Rick and I stood there dumbfounded, neither of us totally sure what had just happened. For two weeks we came back to camp every day, and there was still no sign of Grandfather.

At this point, Rick was about to kill me. To add insult to injury, I got so angry at that bird that when we first returned to camp to see if Grandfather had returned, I went into the lower swamp and I found the bird I had been too lazy to track in the first place. It turned out the bird was a domestic canary that had escaped from my aunt's house three weeks before. No wonder its song had sounded so familiar to me.

Seeking the answer to a question through self-discovery, exhausting every path in search of the truth of the matter, is the kind of passion Grandfather demanded. A coyote teacher will not give you anything. You go to coyote teachers and ask them a question and they will either ask you another question in return or point you in the direction of the answer, leaving it up to you to find the answer yourself.

When a coyote teacher does give instruction on a skill or a form of awareness, we had to take the information with a grain of salt and not accept the teaching at face value. Oftentimes, a coyote teacher would purposely leave something out, so we'd have to discover the missing piece before we could complete the skill successfully. Sometimes he would purposely make a mistake when demonstrating the skill. So we would have to do it and fail until we discovered for ourselves what correction was needed in order to perfect the skill. Not long after I'd met Grandfather, he said to me, "If you believe everything I tell you, you're a fool. Your job is to prove me right or prove me wrong."

Grandfather was very shrewd that way—the way all coyote teachers are. They go to a deeper place within themselves. That deeper place makes a connection to the child, to the adult, whoever the coyote teacher is teaching or wants to (teach or) inspire. The students never realize how they are being drawn in and inspired. In fact the students often think that they are the ones who precipitated this "need" to know when all along it was the coyote who was encouraging it.

Like Grandfather, I am a coyote teacher, except I usually have only seven days per class with my students. The women and men who come to my school quickly learn the days are long, filled with lectures, workshops and exercises, in and around the camp and out in the field. The day starts early and often runs late into the night.

My students have many opportunities to learn and develop a variety of physical and philosophical skills by immersing themselves in the skill itself, rather than listening and taking notes. The one

This picture was taken from the opposite bank of where Tom had his sacred sit spot at Grandfather's main camp. The name "Quiet Waters" stems from the crystal-clear reflective qualities of the pool. It was here Tom watched Grandfather approach the water after a long journey back to camp.
RANDY WALKER

exception to that is the Standard class, in which a lot of information and skills are crammed into one week of teaching. In a future survival situation, a student of the Standard class who had become proficient at the basics of shelter, water, fire and food—the Sacred Order of Survival—would be able to thrive in the wilderness. That student might never return to another class at the Tracker School. Simply to master all the skills taught during the Standard class is to begin a lifelong pursuit of trial and error until experience leads to mastery.

In the majority of the other classes taught at the school, I give the students half an hour to do exercises that Rick and I spent weeks and sometimes months working on. It is then up to the students to put in the time to fully master each skill once they return home. Often I am presenting only the formula or process, and the student must take it from there.

The Advanced Standard class is where students really begin to immerse themselves in working skills. Each student has the opportunity to work on a long-term and a short-term bow. They learn to make arrows and fletchings. They burn out a bowl from a split cedar round and carve a spoon. They have to finish their newly made bowl and spoon by lunch Tuesday in order to be served the stews that are the main meals throughout the week. Flint napping of stone and glass is demonstrated, each person collects and carves a bident or trident tip to be attached to a fish spear and forty-eight new primitive traps are taught. Another big project is building a debris hut that will be slept in by midweek as well. Needless to say, the week is a busy one, heavy on skills. In other words, years of work and skills are presented that week, leaving it up to the students to master each one in their own time.

As I experience the state of the world today, seeing so many things spinning out of balance, I feel a greater sense of urgency to pass on these skills. Only having a week at a time with my students, I am being more explicit about how certain skills work, spelling out things much more than when I first began the school.

In the early 1980s, I invited a group of students to participate in an experimental class that met several times a year for several years. This group of students provided me the chance to see if they could learn Grandfather's advanced teachings. The success this group of students had was amazing, and they became the first medicine society I formed: Coyote Thunder, named after Grandfather's great-grandfather. When any of my Coyote Thunder members return to help out with classes, they sometimes complain that I'm just handing new students information and knowledge that they had to strive and struggle to obtain. My passion to pass on as much as I am able to of what Grandfather taught me is what drives me every day.

These days feel different to me in that time feels short, and I want to reach as many people as possible in these troubling times. For the past seven years, I have been working relentlessly to teach and share as many of Grandfather's physical and philosophical teachings as possible.

Grandfather was a visionary, and he foretold many of the challenges humankind and the Earth face today. On a dark night with the stars shining brightly in the sky, on top of what we call Prophecy Hill, he shared with Rick and me some of the possible and probable futures he foresaw. We sat with him around a small fire as he shared some of the challenges we might face in the coming years. Grandfather told us that when holes appeared in the sky, the Earth had then reached a tipping point. He said these words to us when we were eleven years old, several decades before the first hole in the ozone layer appeared over the Antarctic. It wasn't until the second hole in the ozone appeared over the Arctic that this prophecy became complete. Grandfather said that once the holes appeared, it was too late for the Earth to be healed in a physical manner; it now must be healed in a spiritual way.

My vision for this book and my hope for the future are to present how each person can make a positive difference and learn to go beyond the role of a caretaker, by embracing the role as a healer of the Earth. This book is about the power and importance of the individual. Through experiencing deeper, more expansive ways to connect with the natural world, learning to listen to her voice and feeling her communications, you also experience how the Earth provides you healing in return.

Grandfather believed that if you lead one person back to the Earth, in doing so, that person will lead another, and they another and so on. The individual, through positive action, has an exponential effect on healing the Earth.

FROM MY PERSPECTIVE (RANDY)

I was forty-two years old when I first came to the Tracker School and took the Standard class in 1992. During that week my life changed in a big way. Since my teens, I had been searching for a philosophy of living I could fully embrace. During my search I had been drawn to explore many different philosophies and belief systems. I read about the Eastern philosophies of India, China and Tibet. In college I learned how to cast the *I Ching* with the yarrow sticks, learning not only the philosophy of the hexagrams, but how the synchronicity of the particular hexagram related to that moment in my life. The teachings of Meher Baba were a strong influence in my early twenties and to this day. I took a course in Silva Mind Control, the power of positive thinking, and it strengthened my belief system that we are more than our physical bodies. I thought it interesting that Tom recommended that his students read José Silva's book on Silva Mind Control and had the members of Coyote Thunder take the course or read the book. All of these different ways of viewing the world we live in enriched my life, but something was missing. When I listened to Tom talk about Grandfather in my Standard class, I knew in a visceral manner that my search was over.

By the middle of the week of my Standard class, I knew I wanted to take every philosophy class I could and also the required classes that led to taking a Scout class.

As a child, I had always been fascinated by the indigenous people of North America and their ways of living with the Earth. In grade school I must have checked out this one book on Indian Sign Language from the local library a dozen times. I could totally understand why Tom was so excited and happy to learn from Grandfather, while about a hundred miles south, I was running around the woods, playing Indians by myself. Even though my father's father was part Powhatan, I was brought up in a suburban middle-class setting and had no idea of any Indian lineage until adulthood.

When Tom talked about Grandfather's Worlds of Spirit during my Standard class, it all made perfect sense to me, and I felt I had to learn more about them. When Tom talked about the Apache scouts and what they stand for as the eyes and ears of the tribe, the protectors of the clan and people, it was like my dreams had come true. The idea that I could learn to move like a shadow and master the expertise with the skills they achieved drew me like a magnet.

The next three Februarys, I took Philosophy I, II and III, leaving a year in between each class to further integrate the teachings with what Tom calls "dirt time." Dirt time means working on skills, overcoming walls that impeded my progress and gaining experience.

During that time, I began to experience life in new ways that deepened my connection with Grandfather's Worlds of Spirit. By the summer of that third year I had taken my first Scout class. At the end of the Standard class, after revealing some of the basic truths of tracking and awareness, Tom tells students to take one more look at the Earth because they will never see it the same way again. Of course he was right, because after returning home, each time I would enter the woods near my house, a new world opened its doors to me. I was able to see all the animal runs, big and small. I saw where the deer bedded down or where the porcupines were living high in an old oak tree, their droppings in a pile beneath it.

Professionally, I was working as a family therapist in a thirty-bed, coed, intensive-treatment center for adolescents. The six years before that, I did home-based family therapy with at-risk youths and their families who were court-ordered to be provided counseling. I'd been working in human services for ten years at that point and continued in that field for the next twenty years. The previous seventeen years, I was the executive director of a small nonprofit working with pregnant and parenting at-risk youths who were either court-ordered to placement or living in the greater community. Throughout my journey as a family therapist and working with adolescent youths, the awareness and tracking skills Tom taught, along with the philosophy lessons, helped me immensely in my work as a therapist and staff supervisor. It was like each class I experienced at the Tracker School deepened my ability to be in the moment and to be able to listen to my feelings.

In my early years at the Tracker School, I was able to take two or three classes a year. With a young daughter and son, it was hard to get away a lot. In 1994, we welcomed a third child. With so much going on in my family life, I really had to juggle my schedule.

All the while, I was taking Grandfather's teachings that Tom relayed to us and putting them to use in my everyday life and my professional one.

Today, I am retired, my children are all adults and I am blessed in being able to help out at the school and with the online classes. Now I feel honored that Tom has asked me to help him put this vital book together, furthering Grandfather's vision of doing for our Earth Mother what she cannot do for herself—a vision I and my many brothers and sisters in the Tracker family have embraced as our own.

I have experienced firsthand the role of caretaker and healer of our Earth Mother. Caretaking is something I do to nurture the environments I pass through. It is often like a dance or a moving meditation, interacting with the world of nature, aware of what is and what is not in a state of balance.

One spring morning when I was alone in the Primitive Camp, I decided to walk to the Porta-Johns. It was a good thing going to the bathroom was not urgent. As I wandered through the back paths, I began to caretake the branches that had fallen from the pine trees during the winter and were pushing down blueberry bushes, scrub oaks and other plants along the path. It was early spring and the buds on the scrub oak and blueberry bushes were barely beginning to open.

About an hour and a half later, I completed what was normally a five-minute walk to the bathroom. I had been so caught up in the moment, I'd lost all sense of time and place. When I'd finished my walk, there were five or six different piles of branches along the paths through the blueberry bushes, pine trees and scrub oak. I continued to add to these piles of branches as the weeks went on. A feeling of being connected to each plant and tree around me grew as I moved, back and forth, in slow motion, snaking my way through scrub oak branches to reach a fallen pine branch, taking side trips away from my final destination. Traveling in slow Earth Time had taken me to a place where time seemed to lose meaning—a place where I felt my movements become part of a flow. I had lost my sense of having a destination. Afterward, I had that feeling deep inside me of a job well-done, but more than that, the experience was yet another affirmation to me that Grandfather's worlds are real.

Throughout the book, at the ends of chapters or where appropriate, I will write in my own voice, from the point of view of my experiences at the Tracker School and how Grandfather's teachings enrich my everyday life. I hope to present another perspective on Grandfather's teachings through my eyes, as I share my experiences learning from Tom as my teacher.

Working on this book with Tom is a privilege I never take for granted. Tom has provided the overall concept, the information to be conveyed, the stories and his vision for this book. My role has involved integrating this information into experience, taking notes, doing research, recording new stories and relistening to stories heard many times in past classes so this narrative form can be written. Being in the position to ask Tom questions and fill in parts of stories and experiences he has never revealed before has been a rare honor.

INTRODUCTION

This book comes from the teachings of an extraordinary human being. Stalking Wolf is the name of the man I quickly came to call Grandfather. His lineage and people, the Southern Lipan Apache, are themselves equally extraordinary. As a people, they lived as one with the Earth. In a sense, they gave themselves to the Earth. The Lipan lived in small family groups and clans, following what the land dictated, acting to maintain the balance of nature in each environment they inhabited. Their family groups and clans were spread out over thousands of square miles.

Their philosophy of living with the Earth meant that everything in their natural environment was a living part of them. They honored the Earth, giving respect and thanksgiving for all living things. Through living with the land around them as an extension of themselves, the Lipan lived in harmony with the natural world. Not only did the Earth provide the material for their shelters, the food they ate, their clothing and tools, the Earth also provided the soils, clays, medicines and healing herbs used by their healers and shaman. They gave themselves to the Earth, and the Earth provided for all their needs, in large part because they understood what the carrying capacity of the land was.

Grandfather was born into a small clan, spanning several generations, of the Southern Lipan Apache. When Grandfather was about two years old, his mother, father, grandmother and grandfather were killed in a raid by a band of Spanish-Mexicans. Historically, the Apache tribes and clans and the colonial Mexicans lived in a state of conflict long before the United States expanded their intrusion on the Northern and Southern Apache and the Spanish-Mexicans. Stalking Wolf's great-grandfather Coyote Thunder rescued him during the attack and carried him away. Coyote Thunder brought Stalking Wolf up as a member of the Coyote People clan.

Grandfather grew up in the Chihuahua area of northern Mexico. He received his name, Stalking Wolf, at the age of only five years old when, much to the awe and amazement of the Coyote People who watched him, he stalked and touched a wolf on the outskirts of their camp. Stalking a wolf under any circumstances was a dangerous endeavor. For a five-year-old to accomplish this was extraordinary.

Grandfather had two visions he dedicated his life to. His first vision was to wander far and wide in order to seek out all the primitive skills that were universal and worked in any environment. His second vision was to learn the philosophy and healing knowledge of all religions and peoples, to take their scriptures, ceremonies and dogma back to the purity of nature, in order to distill the essential truths of these separate teachings to pure truths. Grandfather sought those truths that provided reproducible results. He also wanted to share the truths he discovered with others so that these primitive skills, healing techniques and philosophies of living with the Earth would be preserved for future generations of the children of the Earth. The sheer volume of skills he amassed still astounds me to this day. It never dawned on me how much he had wandered until I began teaching the skills he had passed on to me.

To give some examples. Grandfather taught us 232 traps; only thirty-two of those traps were Lipan Apache traps. He taught twenty-eight different types of bows; only two were from the Lipan. Grandfather taught us twenty-three ways to make a primitive fire, only two of them from his people. You get the picture. He learned from everyone and everything he encountered. Henry David Thoreau wrote that one out of every three people he met was his teacher. Grandfather believed that each person he met was his teacher, as was each encounter in the natural world.

To say he wandered is an understatement. He didn't go to South America only one time; he journeyed there numerous times in his sixty years of wandering. In my book *Grandfather*, I go into greater detail about his life and the obstacles he pushed himself through to find the common truths he sought.

The second part of Grandfather's vision was to find the common themes from religions and philosophical belief systems he encountered. He then took them back to what he called the Temples of Creation, full primitive survival. Grandfather stripped away all the customs and traditions and shackling dogmas, distilled them down, to discover each pure and simple truth. It is those simple truths that make up the foundation of all the philosophy workshops and classes presented at the Tracker School over the years.

His dedication to those two visions was staggering. Grandfather left his people when he was barely twenty years old. His people knew that for Stalking Wolf to live his vision, he must do so alone, losing contact with the people he loved for long periods of time. Grandfather dedicated his whole life to living his vision, feeling deep appreciation and wonder with each environment he experienced.

With the state of the Earth today, we can only dream of being able to have such a close connection to the natural world around us. That dream can become an ever-growing reality as connections with the natural worlds around you multiply and deepen. Learning to see the world around you through "Grandfather's eyes" is a major goal of this book. Grandfather's acute awareness, on multiple levels, allowed him to know, deep inside, what actions were needed to heal a damaged area and assist its way toward regaining a state of balance. Once his assessment felt complete, Grandfather would methodically make the changes to the landscape in question, bringing back a state of balance and harmony.

Everything in this book about Grandfather's Worlds of Spirit is taught in the Standard class at the Tracker Wilderness and Survival School. In the Standard class, students learn the Sacred Order of Survival—shelter, water, fire and food; a theme this book will also follow.

It is from the perspective of a growing connection with the Earth that an individual will move toward experiencing the natural world with all their senses, learning how to assess and interact with environments that are stressed and in need. Many people in the United States have been discovering new opportunities for creating natural spaces in city, suburban and rural environments. Community gardens have increased by the thousands in cities, suburbs and rural areas over the past few years. Hopefully these natural spaces and gardens continue to increase as more and more people feel drawn to (connect) live with our Earth Mother. There are far too many abandoned strip malls and parking lots, while new ones are being built at an ever-growing rate. Reclaiming even a small portion of land to create a natural space makes a difference.

By understanding what certain plants need, with regard to sunlight or shade, whether they need a lot of water or a little water, one can determine what types of plants will best thrive in that particular space of light and shade. This is especially important in a cityscape with tall buildings that cast their shadows over large areas.

You will begin to recognize a sense inside of you—a feeling that directs you as to how a place or situation feels "right" or feels "not right." Each person internally experiences this feeling of "right" and "not right" in their own way. For some, it's a feeling of release; for others, it's a tightening feeling that is an indicator of what action is the right one to take. That inner feeling can help determine if a disused parking lot would be better suited to be turned into a community garden or a place of plants and brush as an animal habitat and refuge. The more we accept how we are interrelated to all creation as equals, not standing above and apart from nature, the deeper our connections and appreciation for every aspect of the natural world around us becomes.

I was seven years old the first time I saw Grandfather on a streambed, the banks covered with small light-colored stones. I was looking for stones with fossils etched on them, and, it turned out, so was the man on the bank with me. He seemed pretty old, but I had no idea Grandfather was eighty-three years old when I first met him. He was obviously some sort of Indian, dressed in a top and pants made of buckskin, beautifully decorated with beadwork. His hair was braided, and he was wearing moccasins, with some kind of buckskin bag, also decorated, slung over his shoulder, hanging by his side. This man, seemingly from another century, greeted me with a warm smile.

At that moment, I had no idea of what a profound effect our meeting was to have on my life. Neither did I realize, at that time, our encounter was an important element in Grandfather's personal vision—a vision that called to him when he was deep in the jungles of Brazil, directing Grandfather on a journey that brought him to this pebbled bank, with tannin-colored water gently flowing down from the cedar trees upstream.

Grandfather's vision of passing on the physical skills and spiritual truths he had gathered throughout his sixty years of wandering, searching to learn from the elders of all peoples, from the arctic regions of North America to Tierra del Fuego in South America, was made a reality over the next almost eleven years with his two students, Rick and me. Grandfather wanted to teach us a mixture of skills from many cultures and environs. His vision was based on connecting or reconnecting people with the Earth. Grandfather lived as a child of the Earth, and his goal was for Rick and me to learn and embrace the philosophies and skills needed to live as a child of the Earth.

That first day with Grandfather, we went about our respective prospecting in totally different ways. Any stone that caught my attention, I picked up and scanned it, placing the stone back down and picking up another one. I wasn't having a whole lot of luck, finding only a few rocks with any hint of an ancient sea creature etched into them.

Grandfather seemed to move in slow motion. His attention wasn't only on the stones. He watched the birds fly from tree to tree, stopped to watch a butterfly go by while at the same time he seemed to be listening to something. He would pause and gaze at the carpet of stones he had drifted over to; then he would slowly bend down and pick up one stone. He showed me the design imprinted on the rock; it was a fantastic find. We were able to communicate on a basic level, and I asked him how he was able to find such a great fossil on his first try.

Again his radiant smile broke over his face, and he answered by saying in broken English, while holding an open hand behind his ear and motioning with the pebble in his hand, he was listening to the rocks. He called them talking stones. This was my first lesson from Grandfather. He was beginning to show me how he listened to an inner voice and feeling when surveying the stones surrounding us on the bank.

WATER IS LIFE

I quickly learned that Rick, one of my classmates in school, was related to Grandfather, and the two of us were soon spending as much time after school and on weekends journeying to Grandfather's camp in the Pine Barrens as we could. We didn't realize how lucky we were that with so many people moving into the Toms River area, our school, to meet the growing population, was on double sessions. Having an abbreviated school day gave us that much more time to spend with Grandfather.

This routine of hurrying to Grandfather's camp after school every day became a constant in our lives for years to come. Rick and I took advantage of every opportunity to sit at Grandfather's feet and absorb as much of his knowledge of the physical and spiritual skills he chose to teach us. I was living my dream and so was Rick. Neither of us wanted to consider life without Grandfather. I was also fortunate that my parents had no objections to my spending so much time with Grandfather as long as I continued to do well in school and completed my chores around the house.

As the years flew by, Grandfather's lessons grew deeper and more complicated. Rick and I grew proficient at all sorts of skills, from cranking out a coal with a bow drill or a hand drill in pouring rain to making a bow only using rocks for tools. Each day with Grandfather was an adventure in discovery and learning, so when one of the most important lessons I ever learned from Grandfather came, I wasn't even consciously aware how much this lesson meant to me and how badly I needed to experience it.

During my midteens, I felt like something was missing in my life, and I didn't know what it was. What I discovered during my morning sacred time on the edge of the pond I call the Quiet Waters was that I had been growing complacent, taking Grandfather for granted. I had been failing to appreciate the miracles Grandfather encountered in his everyday life. I call that time my lost years.

Certainly I had been passionate in exploring Grandfather's daily lessons, taking each exercise to the furthest limits I could, but something had been lacking. My morning and evening devotions felt hollow sometimes, as if I was going through the motions. My connection with the world of the Force and Spirit had become more situational than a way of living connected to those worlds.

School was almost over, and I'd been working on a plan to spend two weeks with Grandfather and Rick with no outside responsibilities. When I first shared my plan with the two of them, Grandfather asked what I had in mind. Going into full survival was my answer. Grandfather was so excited by the idea, he was hooting and laughing, rolling around. It was amazing; there was a man who lived in a debris hut excited to strip off his clothes and go into a full-survival situation, leaving everything behind.

My schedule was clear, all my chores completed. I was ready to head to camp when Rick called me to say his plans had changed. He said he couldn't spend the two weeks at camp as we'd planned. His father had just let him know he was taking Rick up to Maine. I was upset my best friend would not be joining Grandfather and me, but still, spending the whole two weeks with Grandfather would be a blast.

When I arrived at camp to let Grandfather know Rick was not going to be with us, Grandfather was in the process of packing his medicine bag of herbs and remedies. Grandfather told me he'd received a message from one of his patients in Cape May who was in need of his help, and he was about to travel south and visit him. As I watched Grandfather get ready for his trip, all my expectations about two full weeks with Grandfather and Rick were shattered.

Nevertheless, I decided I would spend the next two weeks by myself, living with the Earth and practicing all the primitive skills I could. During the first week, I was in a state of bliss, tracking for hours on end. Other times I worked on a variety of skills. I rebuilt my debris hut, began a new father-son bow, gathered food when I was hungry and collected clay so I could fire some new bowls. The week had gone well, but I decided to return home the next day. I felt uncomfortable, out of sorts; something inside me felt missing. I needed to know where this feeling was coming from. I figured I'd go home for a week, do all my chores and come back to camp when Grandfather returned.

The next morning, before I left, I first went to my sacred sit area, as it was a rule with Grandfather that every morning at sunrise and every evening at sunset, we would retire to our sit areas for sacred time. I began to give my thanksgiving to the Great Mystery—Usen, the name Grandfather's people used for the Creator—and to Earth Mother, reveling in the soft breeze moving through the cedar trees across the pond and the mirrorlike reflection of the trees and clouds above in the calm water before me. Almost imperceptibly, I began to feel a soft concentric ring approaching where I sat by the large pool of water, fed by the streams through the cedar swamp from the east. For some reason, I didn't move or react—much to my benefit, I soon discovered.

As if materializing out of a fog, Grandfather suddenly appeared, approaching the water in a reverent manner. There was no rush to his step, even though I could see the dust covering his garments and skin. I knew he had to be thirsty after his eighteen-hour walk along the coast with no potable water on his journey. The hot and dry days of the past week seemed to be wearing on him, but even after walking for most of the night, Grandfather still moved toward the water like someone approaching an altar in a great cathedral. Moving up to the edge of the water in a rhythm slower than a normal fox walk, Grandfather just stood there for the longest time, taking in the beauty of that moment.

Then he knelt down with his knees touching the edge of the pool. After letting the soft concentric rings of ripples play themselves out, Grandfather reached down with a single finger and touched the water. There, in some insignificant unnamed stream in the Pine Barrens, he touched God.

I felt his touch deeply in my soul, and suddenly I realized where the "gap" I'd been feeling was coming from, the complacency I'd fallen into over the past year and a half. I'd been taking for granted the deep connection and communication with the Creator and all creation that Grandfather carried with him everywhere he went. Whatever he interacted with, he did so with respect, appreciation and wonder. As I watched him touch the water with such love, the realization of how I had been taking Grandfather for granted exploded in my mind.

After the last drops of water fell from his finger, Grandfather stood up and gazed across the pond to the cedar forest beyond. He stood there for an agonizingly long time. Grandfather then knelt down again and, with his outreached hand, gently caressed the water's surface for a moment, watching the ripples of water die out; then he stood up again, giving thanks to all of creation. Grandfather then knelt again by the water. He dipped his cupped hands into the water, reverently raising them high to the Creator, allowing the water to drip through his fingers and down his arms, tears of appreciation and thanksgiving running down his face. I knew he had to be thirsty after his long journey, but he was in no rush to fill his needs until he had honored the life-giving water. Only then did he cup more water in his hands and sip the water. Each time he drank from the bowl of his hands, it was from that place of thanksgiving from deep within his soul.

In a sense, my world was crashing down on me. On one hand, I felt like a total fool, as if through my lack of awareness, I'd grown complacent to all the deeper lessons Grandfather had taught me since we first met. At the same time, it was a revelation—an affirmation that every teaching and lesson Grandfather had given me over the preceding years was connected to this one moment. A moment he would say existed in the Eternal Now. A place where physics is at a loss for words.

Of course Grandfather knew I was sitting there. He knew my spiritual crisis had been brewing, and as always, he had given me the space to come to the realization on my own. He was reshowing to me how everything comes from our Earth Mother. Yes, the Great Mystery, God by any name, is the focal point of all organized religions and spiritual practices, but when you've been shown a way to interact with the Creator, to touch God, to feel the Light of the Creator, a new dimension of reality is opened. When you make the choice to embrace the energy of all living things you encounter—all of whom, like you, are a part of creation—the line between me and them fades away. Grandfather brought me back into that moment as I watched him touch the Quiet Waters.

Grandfather's touch was his trademark. He taught me "to touch is to know." That knowing he referred to originates from several realities— what I refer to as Grandfather's Worlds of Spirit. An objective of this book is to present ways for anyone who makes the choice to touch the

Earth in new ways, those who are willing to open themselves and learn from the Earth, to determine what healing a particular place needs. First, learning to listen and feel what an area is telling you, and then making a choice to act, to do for the Earth what she cannot do for herself.

IN MY WORDS

In every one of the classes I have taken with Tom at the Tracker School, he makes the point of emphasizing the importance of each day, at sunrise and sunset, to take some time alone, to spend a period of sacred time, a time to revel in the Temples of Creation, to introspect, journey and give thanksgiving. You could sit in a comfortable chair with a view out the window, if possible. Actually, you can choose any spot you feel drawn to where something in the landscape attracts your attention for some reason. I find being outside in a natural setting works best for me. Having a place you use when you're home, where you can watch the seasons change from one to the other, turns into a wonderful teaching tool.

The place I do my sits at home is about a five-minute walk from the house, in a clearing a few hundred yards up a hill, off a trail that continues on up the hill. About fifteen years ago, I spent a couple hours on days I had free time that summer opening up the area, taking out the pine saplings and the tangle of undergrowth. I used loppers to cut the saplings' roots; otherwise everything was done by hand. My intention was to give honor and respect to each tree and plant I cleared. Over the following years I have dug a firepit and built a sweat lodge in this spot. As I neared completion of the project, it felt right to me to leave one two-foot-high hemlock in the center of the area. That little hemlock is now about fifteen feet high and is a great place for the birds to land or the deer to browse from in winter.

———————

For me, sacred time is a time to connect with that moment. A time to enter Grandfather's Worlds of Spirit and to enter into the moment of creation that is going on right now. A time to anticipate the challenges ahead in the coming day and prepare for them. During the evening, the sit becomes a time to reflect on the events of the day, which I had planned for during the morning sit, and to think about what went well or not. I feel how different the intensity of the wake-up morning energy is compared to the approach of night energy in the evening sit. Sometimes I just sit there in wide-angle vision in surrender and wonder. Other times I have a lot of work to do there along with the regular routine I go through.

Of course if you have your own spiritual practice, combining that with morning and evening sits works great. Even if you have no interest in a spiritual practice, but want to help preserve natural spaces and seek to better understand the rhythms of nature, and want to "tune in" to the ebb and flow around you, moments of wonder and awe await you.

When I finally, after almost twenty years, began doing a morning sit on a consistent basis, my life radically changed for the better. Not only did I feel clearer in my head, my general attitude and my emotional balance, but my physical health was a lot better. Because I was connecting with the natural world, each day, her rhythms were further revealed through observing how each day is different; the wind blows hard one day, and with barely a whisper the next. Each day became a new story to experience. When I did a morning sit, I felt better prepared for tasks and personal goals I faced in the day ahead. I felt more in balance, my actions and emotions coming from a centered place.

A big part of spending sacred time out in nature, at the sit area I had felt drawn to, was the observation, insight and appreciation for the birds and animals that moved and interacted around me. I usually put birdseed and broken-up nuts on either side of my chair and soon had the pleasant distraction to contend with as the chickadees, blue jays, red squirrels, chipmunks and many others came around to grab a bite and interact with one another, while I sat there. When the red squirrel caught the chipmunk sneaking in, there were some epic chases.

After a while, I began to place some nuts on my knees, and things got even more interesting. The sound of a chickadee's wings flying by my head became a soothing and special experience. The feel of their tiny feet on my knee felt like a blessing. The red squirrels also got into the act, perching on my knee and munching away. Somehow, earning the trust of my sit-spot friends felt like a major accomplishment and an affirmation that what I was doing had great importance in my life.

Because I was consistent with my daily sits and sacred time, the depth of the moment grew exponentially over time. After my final prayers were done, I'd find myself slowing my pace a lot as I moved back down the hill. There are four birch trees growing together that are special to me; sometimes I'll stop and pause there. The feelings of connection these moments bring seem to break down any separation I feel between myself and the natural world. The chickadees would fly with me as I walked down, landing around me and chirping. I have come to recognize each bird of that little flock by their behaviors and personalities.

It has been through my deepening connections to the natural flows and rhythms of the days and seasons that I have been able to take a long-range look at what around me needs caretaking or healing, and I have felt as if the caretaking I do now happens on an almost unconscious level. I become aware of a need on the landscape and take the actions necessary, or I note what needs attention and return later.

1

THE HEALING

From our earliest days together, Grandfather taught me how to care for the Earth. Grandfather didn't teach this by suggesting the best way to be a caretaker of nature; he taught by example.

One sunny morning, Grandfather, Rick and I were just beginning a journey from the Primitive Camp on a trip to collect a particular herb. Shortly after we began our walk, Grandfather noticed a large pine branch the wind had knocked down onto some huckleberry bushes. He stopped, walked over to it and meticulously, over a twenty-five-minute period, broke it into smaller pieces, scattering them around over a large area. After watching Grandfather for a few minutes, Rick and I asked if we could help him. Grandfather replied, "Watch now." He was hardly ever one for long explanations; he wanted us to observe exactly what he was doing. He wanted us to see which parts of the tree were rotten enough to be crumbled onto the Earth, which parts were to be broken up into smaller pieces and piled up for future animal shelters. He never threw the broken branches to distribute them around the area. Grandfather would find just the right spot for each one. Even after dragging the log, he gently put it on the ground in a way that didn't interfere with the plants growing there. The log also created a good space for an animal burrow.

Grandfather then told us that by his actions, he was feeding the Earth, helping her to break down the decaying pine bark and wood so they could provide nutrients to the plant life and contribute to the soils of life. The small piles of broken-up branches were constructed in good places to be used as shelter for smaller animals. This was one example of how Grandfather taught by example, not by talking about "how to" caretake.

THE CATHEDRAL

When Grandfather first came to the Pine Barrens in the early 1940s, he discovered that tree bandits had cut a large semicircle-shaped swath of cedar trees near where Rick and I later spent so many years of our youth with him. The cedar trees outside of the cut area formed a majestic half ring of tall cedars we called the Cathedral.

He spent many hours caretaking and healing a portion of this area. In a section close to the Cathedral, Grandfather cleared the area of deadfalls and discarded branches and piles of brush. He then opened up channels for the water to be able to again flow through the area, and then he replanted the area with baby cedar saplings. When Rick and I were introduced to the camp more than fifteen years later, the young cedar trees were just over waist high, with a lone stump, midtorso high in the center, like a natural lectern facing the majestic Cathedral of cedars.

The area you had to go through to get to the Cathedral was a mess of deadfall, tangles of brush and slash left over from the tree bandits. I would have to weave my way through, ducking under bent branches and avoiding tangles of greenbrier on the way to the Cathedral, the place where Grandfather eventually taught us what he called tree preaching. That area of tangles and slash was an example of what the entire place had looked like before Grandfather reclaimed the area, preparing it so that in the coming years, a healthy cedar swamp would once again thrive there.

The Cathedral area was a place of beauty. There was a sacred feel to it with the tall cedars creating a place of quietude, the only sounds being the birdsong and the wind whispering through the high branches.

Later that day, Grandfather showed me a third, very different area, as a way to demonstrate the importance of caretaking. We had come upon a place where many years before, a large tree had fallen onto two growing pine trees. The large fallen tree had lain on the pine trees until it naturally decomposed. The effect on the two pine trees was dramatic. The two thirty-foot trees were misshapen and bent in odd, even grotesque angles. Their growth-stunted and diseased areas showed where the fallen tree lay on the trunks and branches. Grandfather said to Rick and me, "I not here to caretake when this happen." Sometimes seeing the results of where a healing is not undertaken is more powerful than seeing the positive results of caretaking.

Grandfather constantly, through these examples and many others, stressed the importance and effectiveness of seemingly small acts resulting in long-term positive effects on the land. He said it was not only enough to be a caretaker when collecting, one had to be a healer of the Earth as well.

The word for "tracking" in Grandfather's language is also the same word for "awareness." Tracking and awareness are interlinked, to the point that awareness comes from reading the tracks and you become aware of tracks from choosing to be aware of your surroundings. Grandfather could look at a track and tell you what kind of animal

Tom learned tree preaching from Grandfather in a similar grove of cedars. Notice how even at midday the light streams down from above, like it would in a cathedral.
RANDY WALKER

had made that track, if it was male or female, how old the track was, the physical and emotional well-being of the animal and much more. In addition, Grandfather's awareness was on many levels, physical and spiritual, expanding out, sometimes, for miles.

Grandfather's awareness of his surroundings drew him to where and what needed caretaking or healing. He would act to accommodate any imbalance, big or seemingly insignificant, with an attitude of awe, thanksgiving and respect. He believed that no act of caretaking was too small. Each positive action built upon itself, creating a dynamic that grew exponentially. He believed that we are all connected through what he called the Spirit That Moves In and Through All Things.

GRANDFATHER AND I TOOK A
WALK TO THE DOGBANE PATCH

Grandfather and I were sitting by the fire one morning, about three fingers (an hour) after sunrise. Grandfather's people did not have clocks; they used the movement of the sun to measure time. They would hold their hand out toward the sun and measure its passage by the time it took to move one or more fingers of time. On this day, I was nine years old, about two years into my apprenticeship with Grandfather.

He asked me if I would like to take a walk with him to the dogbane patch, which was a bit unusual because, not wanting to miss anything, I already followed Grandfather everywhere he went. Sometimes he had to wave Rick and me away, yelling that he was just going into the bushes to urinate.

So I knew something was up, and I went on full alert. I expanded my awareness and was resolved to observe everything we passed on the short walk. At the time, Grandfather was working on a quad braid, using four different types of cordage. He'd run out of dogbane, so he needed to collect some more stalks.

We slowly fox-walked to the dogbane patch, taking about twenty minutes to get there. Grandfather collected four stalks, taking his time, praying for each plant and letting it know how it was going to be used. Then we made our way back to camp.

Once back, Grandfather asked me, "What did you see?" Well, boy, was I ready. I spent the next thirty minutes describing in great detail everything I had observed during the walk. I talked about the fox that had crossed and recrossed the path the night before, about the newly broken branch on an oak tree from a storm earlier in the week. About the rabbit that had run away when the fox had arrived. I described the state of certain plant life, the different colors of mosses I'd seen and so on until I had exhausted all I'd observed.

Then I made a big mistake. I still almost regret asking the question, but I did. I said, "So, Grandfather, what did you see?" It was late morning when Grandfather began to relate what he had seen on the walk. After the first hour or so, I began to wonder if we'd taken the same walk together. It was like he was describing a different planet from the one I was on. His levels of awareness were so vast and, at the same time, interlocking. How this man saw so much as he slowly walked by left me in a state of awe. Every shift of the wind was mentioned. He referred to the recent animal tracks and ones made in the past month or so. How the track personalities showed two particular foxes had been using a section of the trail on a regular basis. He described things he had no business being aware of unless he had belly-crawled by them.

At dusk, as we made dinner and sat by the fire, I was getting sleepy, and Grandfather still was describing what he'd observed during our walk. His dissertation still had not reached the place of the dogbane patch when I drifted into sleep.

I felt so beat-up and humiliated the next morning when I awoke. After spending time in my sacred sit spot, I walked back to the same path Grandfather and I had taken the day before. I was on my hands and knees, proving out all I could remember of Grandfather's observations. He had been right about everything he'd said. I suddenly realized that he had been describing each plant and bush that grew along the path, the individual ones and the family groups. He'd observed each patch of moss, the thickness of the pine needle cover, what birds had called and when in the journey.

After I'd been on the trail for about an hour, Grandfather suddenly appeared out of nowhere, something he did on a regular basis. He asked me, "So did you prove me wrong yet?" The answer of course was a resounding no—everything I'd remembered of what he'd described had been proven out 100 percent.

For me, that was a difficult lesson to accept, but that walk with Grandfather continues to teach me today. As the years passed and my skills and awareness grew, I continuously pushed myself to not only see what was in my environs, but to feel them as well.

As we all need to be in a healthy state emotionally and physically, so too the Earth needs to be in a balanced state. As all indigenous peoples around the world hold as a truth, Grandfather believed that every entity on the Earth is alive, that it has its own identity and purpose. He referred to water as Earth Mother's blood, the rocks as her bones, the wind as her voice.

If you have an infected wound on your arm, it affects your entire body. You might run a fever from the infection raising your temperature; your mental processes might feel sluggish. Your energy level is low, and your body craves rest and recovery to help heal the infection.

That analogy is true for the Earth today, except instead of one infection, there are thousands upon thousands of ways humankind continues to put stress on the land, seas, waterways and air. When one part is suffering, the entire organism becomes sick. Healing the Earth and restoring balance to the environment were a major part of Grandfather's vision.

When I started the Tracker School in 1978, it was to carry on the vision I shared with Grandfather, teaching other like-minded people ways not only to interact with the Earth in a positive manner, but to heal the places that have been put out of balance through the indiscriminate taking of resources and pollution in all its forms.

When you go on a long sailing trip, you learn that your supplies are limited. Between ports of call, pretty much all you have is on the boat. If supplies run low, you ration what food and water you have. We, as a society, need to move toward this lifeboat mentality. Our supplies onboard—like clean air, drinkable water, forest cover, fish populations in fresh water and our oceans—seem to be diminishing quicker than we ever imagined possible. Worldwide food shortages are a constant, with a third of the world's population going to bed hungry each night.

Mahatma Gandhi once said, "Earth provides enough to satisfy every man's need, but not every man's greed." A major test we all face today is a change in our consciousness toward preserving the natural resources around us; not thinking of them as commodities that, once harvested or mined, will make us richer. It's a consciousness change that is the opposite of "He who dies with the most toys wins." If our conscious attitude is to seek ways to lessen our "footprint" in the ways we live, we'll use fewer resources and share more of what we have with others. Small acts like combining a number of errands to run all at one time when making trips to town will cut down on the gas burned and wear and tear on the environment.

Let's face it, folks. Our Earth Mother, our home, is in trouble. She provides us the material for our shelters, the water we drink, the air we breathe, the food we eat and the fires that warm us. We are seeing firsthand her resources dwindle as oceans warm, potable drinking water becomes scarcer and air becomes increasingly polluted. This is true especially around cities and industrial areas where the spread of all sorts of chemicals, industrial pollution and smog infiltrates our environments and bodies.

One of the major problems we face comes from modern man's belief that one can rule the environment, treat it with contempt, extract resources, leave the waste and move on. We, as a human race, must change the way we view and interact with the natural world around us if we care about what kind of world our grandchildren's grandchildren will inherit. We must accept that it is no longer enough to be a caretaker or steward of our natural world; each of us individually must embrace the role of healer when it comes to saving what's left of our Earth Mother. Without her, we have nothing.

This book is a call to action, to affirm that each one of us can effect positive change as healers and children of the Earth. Nothing you do is insignificant. Each time you pick up a piece of trash or lift a fallen branch off the bush bent down under its weight, you are making a positive difference, energetically and physically. Besides positive physical actions, a consciousness change toward how we connect to and interact with our environments, viewing ourselves in relationship to our environment, is key to our survival.

Grandfather stressed to Rick and me how each interaction with our environment, no matter how big or small, sends concentric rings out. These concentric rings make an impact all around us, near and far, through the Spirit That Moves In and Through All Things. Like a pebble dropped into quiet waters, the effects of our actions ripple out. How far these ripples go out would amaze you.

Science has also demonstrated how a small action, like a warmer ocean temperature in one place, can influence future weather patterns thousands of miles away. This is now known as the butterfly effect. In 1961, Edward Lorenz, a professor of meteorology at MIT, was rerunning a computer simulation for a two-month weather forecast using twelve variables. He rounded off one of the variables in the computer program from .506127 to 506. That slight variation had a profound effect on the outcome of the simulation, leading Lorenz to realize how small changes can have great consequences. In 1972, Lorenz was asked by his peers to present his work at the conference of the American Association for the Advancement of Science. His presentation was titled "Predictability: Does the Flap of a Butterfly's Wings in Brazil Set Off a Tornado in Texas?" His presentation inspired scientists from other disciplines to apply his findings to their fields of study. They too reported similar types of results where a minuscule change in one variable could have a major effect on the final outcome. Lorenz's work is another example of how one person's actions, however small they appear at the time, can have a significant effect.

In facing the seemingly insurmountable climate challenges we face today, denial, helplessness and apathy are some emotions we all experience at times. The whole idea that one person's actions can have any effect on the entire Earth can cause a person to feel totally inadequate. It is through honoring and embracing the ecosystems we live in that a person can begin to feel more and more connected to all things. The small acts of love, whether by picking up discarded trash or removing blockages to ease the flow of a stream, build a positive momentum toward balance.

In a recent poll, people were asked if they felt that there was a need for addressing environmental action. It found that 96 percent of the people polled were in favor of taking strong actions, but 91 percent said they supported these actions only as long as those actions did not affect their day-to-day lives.

Well, our lives are already being affected in major ways. Just in the past four to six years, we've experienced storms around the world growing in size and intensity because of warmer oceans and changes in ocean currents and in the jet stream. Instead of a large storm over land moving across a continent, some storms have become stalled, dropping record-breaking amounts of rainfall and causing flooding. Hundreds of millions of people, not to mention animals, trees, crops and waterways, have experienced sicknesses caused by air and water pollution. Recently, a large increase in premature births and babies born with low birth weights was found to be directly linked to air pollution.

I believe that the time for studying the issues we face is over; each one of us is already affected by the climate changes humans have been instrumental in accelerating. Record heat waves and long droughts have occurred on each continent.

The warmest year in recorded history was 2014. Then came an even warmer year in 2015, and then 2016, 2017 and 2018 saw record-breaking high temperatures throughout the year, making them among the warmest years on record. Ocean temperatures rose in 2015 as much as in the previous twenty years combined. Syria's five-year drought and the one that has been going on for four years in the southwestern United States have affected millions of lives. In Syria, the drought drove entire communities into urban areas and was a key factor in the civil unrest that has evolved into a horrific civil war, ongoing as of this writing.

Wars, armed conflicts and civilian oppression have also increased in practically every corner of the world. I could list all the places armies and factions face off against one another, but that's too depressing. It's hard enough keeping a positive attitude when faced by the magnitude of the issues before us. That said, militaries engaged in combat or training are some of our biggest polluters of the environment.

GARBAGE ATTRACTS GARBAGE

In the early 1980s, when I was working with the members of Coyote Thunder, I realized I could teach the way of the spirit Grandfather had handed down from his people and gathered during his decades of wandering. Some of these spiritual truths I teach in the philosophy classes at the Tracker School today. It was the members of Coyote Thunder who pleaded with me and encouraged me to teach these skills to the mainstream Tracker students. Before Coyote Thunder was formed, I had only taught the physical skills of survival, not Grandfather's way of the spirit.

At one of our meetings, we tried an experiment. We left a bag filled with garbage on a well-traveled sandy road in the Pine Barrens. When we returned a week later, other people had dumped enough garbage to fill half a pickup truck. When we then returned several days later, there was enough garbage dumped to fill a whole pickup truck. After we cleaned the area of garbage, no one dumped their trash there anymore. Even one piece of trash discarded on a trail is like an invitation to other people to throw away their own trash. It can work the other way as well.

Years ago, I was at Wells Mills Park with two of my sons, River and Coty, to give a short talk at an event celebrating Christmas for the Animals, an annual event put on by a nonprofit organization I helped form, stemming from Grandfather's vision.

The goal of the Children of the Earth Foundation (COTEF) is to teach children the Sacred Order of Survival through games and activities and bring these children closer to the Earth. There are weeklong camps held in the summer and workshops throughout the year that are designed for children from the age of four years old to seventeen years old.

It was a cool December day. The skies were blue with cotton ball clouds slowly drifting across the sky; a light breeze was whispering through the pines, rising to a gusty wind now and then. People of all ages had come to make peanut butter pinecone treats, string together garlands of popcorn for the wildlife and see demonstrations of different primitive skills. People were milling around the park, enjoying the day. The smell of burned cedar from the bow drill workshop filled the air along with the smell of freshly made popcorn.

After I gave my short talk and thanked all who had come to help give the local wildlife a better chance to survive the coming winter, and told some stories about Grandfather and his vision of bringing people back to the Earth, I was walking around the park with my sons. Coty saw a paper wrapper that was blowing across the open space; he ran over and picked it up and then another stray paper and another until his hands were full. As he walked over to the nearest trash can to throw it away, people near him had noticed his actions, and they too began to look around for trash to pick up. All of a sudden, it seemed, other children and adults young and old began picking up pieces of paper and trash that was being pushed around by the breezes. In a very short time, the grounds were clear of any trash. There was a new feeling of satisfaction and accomplishment felt by the people in the park. It seemed easier to smile and a sense of community was shared between the young and old.

This is an example of one small action leading to a greater action. It also shows that no matter how small someone is, they can be a positive force for change. That day at the park when Coty picked up that piece of litter, he was three years old.

MY FATHER AND THE STREAM

The last person on Earth I thought would embrace the concept of conservation and sensitivity to the Earth and the environment was my father. I never understood how he and Grandfather could sit talking and laughing for hours on just about any topic and be such good friends, because my father was old-school. He was an engineer from Scotland. Everything to him was about industry, development and work. He could fix any type of machine and figure out how to build whatever we needed around our small house.

When my son Tommy was four years old, we were living up at the old farm where I ran many of the Tracker classes. He and I were heading down to the Primitive Camp to prepare for an advanced class. On the way down, I asked Tommy if he wanted to stop in and see Grandpa and Grandma. Of course he was thrilled and said so.

We arrived at my parents' North Jersey house on a hot August day and spent a few hours catching up with my parents. It was then my father shocked the heck out of me by asking if he could come down to camp with us. Naturally I said that was a great idea, looking forward to Tommy and me getting to spend some quality time with him.

We were coming down into this area, approaching the camp where the road paralleled a stream near where we used to live when I was growing up. This stream was about twenty feet across, chest deep in places with beautiful crystal-clear water with just that slight hint of Pine Barrens' tannin in it. All of a sudden, my dad yelled for me to stop the truck. As I pulled over, I thought something in the truck was broken.

Since my father could fix anything, I stopped the truck. My dad jumped out and started unbuttoning his shirt. In an excited voice, he proclaimed to Tommy that this was the exact spot where he had taught his dad, me, to swim. It was also where we had gone to get fresh water whenever there was a power failure and a place we used to go to for family picnics. Essentially, a special place in our family's heart.

By now, Tommy and I were out of the truck, while my father was painting this beautiful picture of the swimming area. My dad said to Tommy, "Let's go. Let's swim in the stream," but Tommy replied, "We can't, Pop."

He was only four years old, and yet he was telling my father we couldn't go in the water. My dad looked questioningly at Tommy and asked, "Why not?"

Tommy explained that the water was sick.

"What do you mean the water is sick?" my father asked. "The water's clear."

He stated again that this was where we always used to get water to drink, where Tommy's dad had learned to swim.

Tommy told his grandpa to look at the vegetation along the edges of the stream. Now, for a four-year-old, "vegetation" is a big word. My father's gaze traveled up and down the stream banks as far as he could see. and sure enough, all the vegetation along the banks was dead. Even though the water appeared clear and fresh, something in the water had killed all the underbrush along the banks.

Tommy observed that there were no fish left, no turtles sunning on the rocks. My father looked at us with horror on his face and asked, "Why?" Tommy pointed in the distance to a hill. There are basically no hills in the Pine Barrens, so where he was pointing seemed out of context. Tommy then replied, "Because of that damn dump."

At that, my father lost it. He broke down and began crying. His world came crashing down on him because it was his vote on the city council that had helped put that dump there, in a place it never should have been allowed. The people pushing for the dump knew what it was going to do to the water table, but they never revealed what the long-term effects of placing a dump there would be. By my father's vote, he stole the many chances to experience the wonder and beauty of that natural place from his grandchild. I remember him saying, "My God, what have I done?" Here was a man in his sixties saying, "How much time do I have left? Ten or fifteen years? How much time does the Earth have left today?" My father was never the same man after that, never, ever the same.

TWO APPROACHES TO SURVIVAL

A lot of people ask, Isn't being a survivalist like being a swarm of locusts that descends on the landscape and virtually devours everything? As a survivalist, don't you go back into the beautiful Temples of Creation with nothing and take things from the landscape to survive? You have to kill things—be it plant, animal or rock. And you imagine, "Wow, it's kinda like that swarm of locusts eating everything in their path." Well, yes and no.

Grandfather was very quick to point out to me there are two philosophies of survival. One he called the white man's survival. The other he called native survival. He said the problem is that the white man's survival is what is wrong with the Earth today.

Let's take a Native American man or woman and an early white explorer, surveyor or trapper. The fur trapper wakes up one morning and says to themselves, "I'm running low on musket balls and powder. I'd better build myself a bow." So he rides out on the landscape, searching out the open fringe areas of the landscape where forest meets field or field meets stream, because he knows that there grow the tallest, straightest and truest of the saplings. In short order he finds one and cuts it down with no thought, no care. Never satisfied with just one, he cuts another, just in case he finds a hidden flaw in the first one. He doesn't care what he does to the landscape. He doesn't realize that cutting a sapling from a fringe area is the worst thing you can do. He doesn't even consider how his actions will affect his children and grandchildren to come. Nature is there for his convenience. It's his to use and his to abuse. After all, it says in the good book, we have lord and dominion over the beasts and the Earth. In his mind, nature is there to use and abuse. Grandfather summed that type of survival up. He said we are a society of people who kill our grandchildren to feed our children.

This is the alien survival, the struggle of the humans imposing their will on the environment and taking whatever they please, destroying the ecosystems in the process. Yes, that is the swarm of locusts Grandfather was referring to, but that's not the type of survival consciousness we need.

Then there is the other type of survival. Native men or women awake and decide they need to make bows. They fast, they pray and they purify themselves. They consult with the elders and firmly establish an extreme need. Then they go out to the landscape, taking their time, feeling what areas they are drawn to. They bypass the fringe areas that they encounter. They are looking for a place in the forest that is at war. A place that was killed by a wildfire or landslide. They search for a place in the forest where there is a sea of saplings, all fighting for sunlight, space and water. The native people know that most of those trees are going to die in their quest for survival, and the trees that are left could become gnarled and disease ridden. They look for a place where a bunch of saplings are growing close together, vying with one another for limited resources. The native men or women know that through the saplings' struggle for existence, they will be stronger, tougher from the experience. Bows made from those saplings will have a much stronger snap and throw than saplings from the fringe area that have never experienced that kind of struggle to survive.

They search the area for just the right saplings that are dying or dead and, even if dead, that once taken from the clump of their brothers and sisters, space will be created for the others to become stronger.

The traditional Indians or people who approach the situation in a native way ask themselves, "If I take this tree, what will I do to the landscape now? Will I make it better? Will I open the landscape so that other trees can grow up strong and true?" If that question is answered positively, they will then ask what will they leave for their children and grandchildren? Will they leave them a strong and healthy forest? Or one that is sick and dying? And when that is answered positively, they will make contact with the sapling and say a prayer in their hearts, something like this:

Little sister, please forgive me, as I am taking your life, and a part of mine, in order to help my people live. You will help my people grow strong and live in a good way, a way that helps my people live in harmony with our Earth Mother. I will honor your death by making a bow to feed my people in a sacred way. Each scrape of rock on your skin will be done with thanksgiving in my heart. From deep in my heart, I thank you for your sacrifice. It is done.

Then and only then will the person living with the Earth cut that sapling with the greatest care, reverence and appreciation.

Part of the survivalists' purpose is to notice what is needed that will heal and benefit the Earth. If you follow this law, you will be given what you need from your environment. You will feel drawn to the resources you need for survival as well as toward the areas on the landscape that would become healthier from your attention. It is a clear give-and-receive type of interaction.

If you disregard this law of balance, you will suffer for it, as what you need will not be provided to you without great effort. Finding the resources for your immediate needs will turn into a battle rather than an intimate conversation.

The survivalist, then, in that consciousness, becomes a tool of the Creator, a caretaker of the land, a steward, a healer. For whatever a survivalist takes, it makes the land better.

CONCLUSION

I approach the healing of the Earth from the perspective of a survivalist: promoting the survival of the Earth and also our own survival. The Earth could probably survive without humankind and the impacts on her we have made. The same is not true for humankind; we cannot live without the Earth. I believe our present situation is that serious. This means I approach healing the Earth through the philosophy of the Sacred Order of Survival: shelter, water, fire and food. In a survival situation, if you take care of your needs in the above order, you have a far better chance of not only surviving, but living in relative comfort. Depending on the situation, sometimes fire and water are reversed, such as if you need fire to purify water, but otherwise, following the Sacred Order of Survival will keep one alive if presented with a full-survival situation.

Naturally, there are many wilderness skills that are needed when going into full survival, but anyone can learn the basics. Only by going into full survival for periods of time will you really master those skills.

This book is not about wilderness skills, but it is a vehicle to illustrate how one person, you, if you so choose, can make a real difference through embracing the vision of how to become a healer and a steward of the land. As a survivalist, you can choose not just to survive but to allow your life to make a positive difference in a forest or in your yard. Humans can be catalysts that restore balance to a forest, just as they can choose to destroy it. It all comes down to an internal change in how we view our environment and making the choice to become a positive agent of change. In the following chapters, healing the Earth will be presented from the point of view of the survivalist, by using the Sacred Order of Survival: shelter, water, fire and food. These are doorways into divergent ecosystems, as the needs of these ecosystems depend upon their interaction with all that is around them. Grandfather said it this way, "Whatever you take away from the Earth, you take away from yourself. Whatever you destroy of the Earth, you destroy of yourself."

2

SHELTER

In the big picture, spaceship Earth is our shelter—shelter being the land from the ground up and sometimes, as with caves, deep into the Earth. The forests, the fields, the plains and the deserts are all forms of shelter. These places are shelter not only for humankind, but for all animals, birds, insects, fish and amphibians in one form or another. But it doesn't stop there; all plants and trees work together to provide shelter for one another in a balanced ecosystem. Plants and shrubs will also use the landscape as a form of shelter, like a family of berry bushes thriving behind a bluff that protects them from the strong winds.

Take a cedar swamp in perfect balance. When you look at it from above, you see how it forms a domelike shape. The older grandfather and grandmother trees are in the center, with the younger trees growing around them, progressively younger and smaller trees, moving out to the seedlings on the edges of the swamp. This dome shape creates a buffer from the wind, the whole forest working together to disperse heavy winds when they blast out of the west or the northeast across the Pine Barrens.

Take away the balance of the cedars and cut a large swath through

This section of the cedar swamp was cut down in the late '90s. Note how the edge of the cedar forest has many fallen and dead trees from the lack of a protective "dome" structure protecting the old growth from the winds and storms.
RANDY WALKER

the natural state of growth, and the cedars lose their naturally formed windbreak; their integrity as a complete entity is disrupted. Over time, the edges of the clear-cut area will be littered with falling cedar trees ninety feet high, blown over as the first line of defense to meet the oncoming storms. The streams that trickle and flow through a cedar swamp will be lost in the clear-cut, gone for a generation or more.

How we go about restoring and healing a damaged area, like a clear-cut through a cedar swamp, means looking ahead many years. Learning how to project into the future what needs to happen for an area to regain its balance relies on understanding what the hoped-for outcome will become.

The first cut of the cedar swamp was done in the early '90s. Tom had several Caretaking classes replant cedar trees and open water channels soon after it was cut down. Now there stands a healthy forest of young cedars, some forty feet high.
RANDY WALKER

A little over twenty years ago, during a Caretaking class, sixty students spent one week clearing out slash left from an area of the cedar swamp that had been clear-cut a few years before. Once the slash and the wooden ramp that ran across the cut were cleared out, the students and I created active channels for water to run through the area and planted hundreds of baby cedars, which are today as tall as forty feet high. The students accomplished in one week what would have taken one person six months to accomplish.

Two stories that illustrate the positive effect one or two individuals can make in a particular landscape come from India and China.

Jadav "Molai" Payeng, a man who lives in northeastern India, has been planting trees and shrubbery in this one particular area for the past forty years. When he was sixteen years old, he came upon a large number of dead and dying snakes that had been washed up on a dry expanse of exposed beach by floodwaters rushing down from the Himalayas during the spring melt. In a state of shock, he sat and cried on the beach. Seeing and experiencing such a great loss of life, he felt a passionate need to keep things like the slaughter of these snakes from happening again, and he vowed to do something about it. That area is now called the Molai Forest.

Molai lives on one of the world's largest river islands, Majuli Island, home of one hundred seventy thousand people. Over the past hundred years, the island of Majuli has lost 70 percent of its landmass to the river Brahmaputra's floodwaters, which annually arrive from the Himalayas.

Thirty years after Molai began his project, a sprawling 1,360-acre forest now stands. Molai is also a farmer who has planted crops in one part of the reclaimed forest. The increase in wildlife over the years has been dramatic. The land has become a safe haven for rhinos, deer, Bengal tigers, elephants and a variety of birds. At one point a herd of one hundred elephants inhabited the forest. Molai plans to spend the next thirty years creating another forest.

The second story about the efforts of, in this case, two men who act together as one, comes from northeastern China. Jia Haxia, fifty-four years old, who has been blind since 2000, and Jia Wenqi, who lost both his arms at the age of three when he grabbed an exposed electrical wire, have teamed together for the past ten years, planting trees near their village. Haxia states, "I am his hands. He is my eyes."

Since 2004, they estimate they have planted ten thousand healthy trees, while three thousand of the trees they planted died. At first, their fellow villagers were skeptical, since the barren beach area they chose to plant with trees had been bare of vegetation for years. The villagers didn't believe what they were doing was possible.

Today it's a different story. Since the bare banks of the river are now covered with trees, things have changed. The villagers help them with their project by watering the trees, helping fix their tools and bringing them saplings to plant.

Initially, Haxia and Wenqi wanted to address the issue of the riverbanks eroding. The trees they were planting were to help protect their village from the annual floods. They both tell others, "When we work together, two become one."

These two men believed they could make a difference, even when everyone else doubted them. Against all odds, they made a huge difference, bringing the barren lands around them back into balance and creating healthy living spaces for a multitude of wildlife.

These two stories are about the long-term care of an area, creating healthy, functioning ecosystems that protect and revitalize animal and bird populations as well. Sometimes projects can be short-lived and make a difference as well. Even if a person took care of an acre of land for one year, his or her efforts of increasing the growth of the area by removing dead branches, opening up plants that are crowding out one another and planting seeds, making the area greener and healthier would make a difference even if the next year that land was bulldozed for development. During that one year, the healthier area would put more oxygen into the air; it would provide better shelter and food for the animals and birds. Another benefit would be to the person who did the caretaking. They would learn more about what works best and learn from any failures. Another positive side effect would be through the deeper connections that person made with the land and the sense of satisfaction from giving back to our Earth Mother. The positive impact made on the land, even land then destroyed, is significant.

INDICATORS FOR A HEALTHY AREA

To evaluate a particular environment for healthy animal activity, first look at the vole population. Voles are indicator animals that need cover for protection. There will be a wide variety of vegetation wherever voles are found. Voles, along with mice and moles, are the most sought-after game, by all manner of predators, including wolves, coyotes, foxes, raccoons, weasels and other carnivores. Population-wise, there are more voles on this planet than any other species of animal. A healthy vole population means that the area in which they live is rich in all sorts of animal species.

Several months after meeting Grandfather and visiting him at or

Each circular swirl of grass represents tunneling into the grass from the snow by mice, voles and moles. The many tunnels indicate a healthy ecosystem.
RANDY WALKER

near a place we called the Medicine Cabin, Grandfather took us to visit his permanent camp near Waretown. In past generations this area had been used by the Lenni-Lenape as a camp for their herbalists and healers during their summer migrations because of the rich diversity of healing herbs and medicinals that grew there. There is a well/ spring that we rebuilt in the cedar swamp not far from Grandfather's camp that was first built by the Delaware Indians over three hundred years ago.

On the walk to his camp, we passed a field of grasses, and we paused. Grandfather told Rick and me to look at the field of grasses in wide-angle vision for a while. Wide-angle vision is where you soften your gaze and look just above the horizon without focusing on any

Originally built by the Delaware and the Lenni-Lenape three hundred years ago, Grandfather, Tom and Rick rebuilt the well in the early 1960s. The area of camp was part of an annual migration route to the sea.
RANDY WALKER

one spot, but take in the whole area as one. If you hold your arms out at your sides and expand your vision so you can see your fingers wiggle on both hands, you are in wide-angle vision.

He told us to just watch the field. After a while, a dramatic change occurred; all of a sudden the grasses seemed to open up. I could see trails and runs intersecting through the grasses. Instead of a field of grasses, I knew I was seeing a world of the animals that lived within the field, from the voles and mice runs to where the rabbits and foxes wove through the grasses. There was a hidden world right in front of us. We had never looked at it the right way to see this world before.

Of course seeing voles in the wild is a lot more difficult than discovering evidence of their shelters, their "hiding holes." To discover the extent of an area's vole population, you have to get down on your hands and knees in a grassy place or a high-debris area and look for small entrance holes to their burrows and dig around with your fingers to find the slender channels they use to travel through the vegetation.

One afternoon, Grandfather, Rick and I were sitting in Rick's backyard, enjoying the afternoon. Rick's father was very precise in how he cut and manicured his lawn; it seemed like no blade of grass was out of place.

Something that had been bothering Rick and me for a while was how, when we were sign-tracking with Grandfather, he always could find lots of animal hairs and we could not. I might have found two or three on a good day while Grandfather would have collected twenty-five or thirty in the same period. We asked him what our problem was, and he answered, "Not looking the right way."

This was not long after Grandfather had instructed us to "Go ask the mice." This time he said, "Go ask the lawn." Grandfather said to look from the majestic to the minute. At first I was hesitant, not believing a lawn so perfectly cut could hold any natural secrets, but was I wrong.

It was around two o'clock in the afternoon when we began to explore the lawn and see what it might teach us. The two of us became so immersed in the miniature worlds revealed to us, we were still at it when it became too dark to see. We then got out Rick's flashlights, and only the batteries running down ended our fun.

There was so much to see in that tiny world. At one point, I imagined myself shrunk down to the scale of the grass landscape, and I determined where I would build a shelter on the top of this "cliff." As I was imagining the building of the shelter, Grandfather came by and pointed to the cliff I'd been fascinated with. He showed me that I was really looking at a rabbit track made from its right hind foot.

That afternoon taught us to look at the smallest detail, getting down on our knees or bellies and picking through the blades of grass, finding vole and mice runs, their scat, even hairs. We began to find more animal hairs than ever before!

Later Grandfather said if that was just a lawn, imagine everything else outside of the lawn. Not only had our world gotten a lot smaller in observing details; it had grown exponentially larger, because we knew how much more might be found in the wild grasses or in a blueberry patch growing out of a thick cover of debris.

IN MY WORDS

In Vermont, in the winter when there's snow cover, the tracks of the foxes and the cats weave across the field behind my house. It's easy to see the hunting patterns evolve and where the predator has been digging down into the snow to catch the vole or the mouse in the tunnel under the snow. Sometimes there is evidence of a kill, where there's blood on the snow. These under-snow tunnels are the only way the voles, mice and moles can move around during the coldest times of winter; they serve as their corridors to the bark and leftover foliage. This way of winter travel is established because the ground, their normal way of tunneling, is frozen hard, several feet deep.

In the spring, as the snow melts, the winter tunnels of the "mice people" make patterns on the field like waves ending their run on a beach, leaving a subtle line from the limit of each wave's reach. Seeing these impressions in the snow is also an indicator of the strength or weakness of the vole population in a particular area.

LEARNING THROUGH OBSERVATION

Grandfather's people have descriptions for the power and energy each cardinal direction represents. When he would call in the direction of the south, Grandfather would softly speak these words out loud or to himself:

Grandmother of the South

Place of hard work and soft summer rains, teach us to grow as your saplings do, with your feet rooted firmly in the soils of life, and your arms reaching toward the wisdom of the Sun. Teach us the wisdom of your mice people, to live close to the Earth and find the Grandeur in the smallest details that people only find in the Grandest vistas.

Grandfather's awareness was so expansive, and every day we were with him, he constantly surprised us with his knowledge of what was going on around him. Rick and I were determined to discover how

44

Grandfather did it. How was he so aware? We decided we were going to follow his every move, every glance he made at his surroundings to see if we could find new clues to how he was able to see and know all he revealed to us about each area we passed through.

One of us would be the "caller" and watch everywhere and everything Grandfather was looking at. When I was watching his actions, I'd say, "He's looking up to the left, forty-five degrees. He's looking down and to the right," and so on. Rick would then look to where I reported and take in every detail. Then we would switch roles, and later, we would compare notes.

Just like in "Go Ask the Mice," we learned through observation—one of us watching Grandfather and the other looking where he was looking. So when Grandfather said to us, "Don't disturb it," at first we had no idea what he was referring to. For the past twenty minutes, Grandfather had been walking along in a slow fox walk, hands behind his back and looking down.

Rick and I looked near and far, but couldn't find anything that we might disturb. Grandfather thought this was really funny. He was laughing quietly a few dozen feet up the trail. After several agonizing minutes scanning all around us, Rick leaned back against an old pine tree and took a deep breath. As he did so, he looked up at a branch just above his head. On the branch was an old, graying female great horned owl.

Where had Grandfather gotten that information? He'd been looking intently at the ground for the past twenty minutes or so. How had he known the owl was on the branch? The trail we were walking down was fairly wide, bordered by some scrub oak, blueberry bushes and greenbrier, with the trees being predominantly pines. There was a light cover of debris on the sandy path, a perfect place to track.

When we asked him how he had known the owl was there, he said to us, "Go ask the mice." So we did, for months on end, lying on our bellies, interpreting mice tracks. I even got calluses on my sternum from lying on the ground so much.

This lesson was a turning point in my life. Not only did I learn how the mice acted when there was an owl around. I learned how the mice reacted when a fox or a weasel was around. I learned how the fox reacted when there was a coyote around or when deer were in the area. We were beginning to see how each trail of tracks we followed showed that particular animal's reaction to the animals around them. We also discovered the many types of shelters the prey would seek when being hunted. Rick and I began to get a feeling for the interconnectedness of all the animals around us. We'd never realized the extent to which each track, from whatever animal, showed how the many strands of life around us were connected through the tracks.

When prey is threatened, it seeks shelter, refuge. The fox will chase the mouse into its hole or burrow and try to dig it out, going as deep as eight inches down. How soon an animal reaches shelter and to what extent their shelter protects them determines if they live or die. For us, then, shelter took on a whole different meaning. Trees also became a form of shelter for Rick and me when we had to avoid the packs of wild dogs that roamed the Pine Barrens, but the mice people constantly had to be aware of danger and where their escape routes were when out collecting food or materials. In a ten-square-foot area, a mouse might have seven or ten different holes and burrows to run to when danger approached.

Some animals are shelter builders. Birds build many types of nests in which to hatch and raise their young. The squirrel family builds a shelter or nest. It was squirrel nests that Grandfather used to teach Rick and me the basic fundamental truth for building a debris hut, the preferred shelter outside of any long-term living situation. That truth is dead-air space. The fluffy arrangement of the leaves and the intertwined twigs traps the squirrel's body heat inside the shelter and the dome shape sheds the rain, keeping it dry inside.

Beavers are possibly the most well-known shelter builders. The beaver has been a strong totem in many Native American tribal clans throughout history. Beavers are known for their industriousness; but modern society often sees beaver dams as nuisances when waterways become blocked. Their shelters usually have an entrance below the water, where they tunnel up into the dry part of the shelter that rises above the water. Not many predators are able to follow beavers into their lodges.

Mice like to find soft things in their environment to take home and "furnish" their burrows. Have you ever had a mouse "problem" in your house and opened a drawer or a box that had been unused for a while? You might have found all types of material and stuffing combined to make a fluffy shelter. The same type of thing is happening underground as well.

The dome and spherical shelters created by animals are used by the indigenous peoples throughout the world. In their cultures, if something doesn't work, it doesn't get passed on to future generations, which is a lesson modern society has not taken to heart.

CARETAKING AND HEALING THROUGH SHELTER

In caretaking, you use the vole population as a starting point. If the area has a strong vole population, you ask what more you might do to help the area thrive. In assessing the vole population, you also take into account the vegetation in the area. Is there a diverse number of plant species, or is it dominated by a particular species?

In an area with a limited vole population, or one where no evidence of them can be found, you might have a starting point for healing the area. If plants of different species could grow there, could they be imported or could seeds be planted?

Other criteria to look for are what I call fringe areas. I look for "islands" of vegetation and cover as a positive indicator. The voles find a rich environment between the hard ground and the leaf litter. By being able to recognize healthy fringe areas, you learn what an unhealthy area or old fringe area needs in order to become replenished and healthy again.

You won't find these islands in the deep forest, as there is not the diversity of vegetation growing under the canopy above. Certain species of animals, like caribou and elk, go on long migrations to reach areas they know will be rich in vegetation when they arrive. Poor vegetation in one area will often cause animals to migrate to another.

Water is another important factor. Usually where there is water, it is a rich vegetation area. The area is biome rich. In assessing an old fringe area, you look to see if there were waterways there. Were the waterways moved or maybe dammed upstream? This is where finding seeps and springs can come in handy. Even seasonal streams can be used to reclaim a fringe area, so be aware of dry streambeds if you are looking at an area in summer or fall.

I think it's ironic that when subdivisions are built, the streets are often named after the trees cut down to clear the area or the animals whose homes and habitats have been destroyed so the houses and roads can be built.

Backyards are natural buffer zones and there are ways to create sanctuaries for the birds and animals who live around your home. Wherever I live, I put out birdseed in bird feeders and/or on a table. After a short while, species after species of birds will come in to feed there. I grow to know the different birds, their habits and peculiarities. They become used to having me around, sometimes landing on my head and shoulders when I take out the can of birdseed to refill the feeders. As I walk out and shake the can of birdseed, the chickadees are already in the tree above, chirping their pleasure.

Another way to help the wildlife is to build brush piles and what I call "brush balls." That's where I take a bunch of brush and weave it into the shape of a ball, tying it with natural cordage that will eventually decay. These are perfect shelters for vole and mouse families that over time break down and return to the soils of the Earth.

Wood is a valuable material we use for shelters and for fires to cook our food, purify our water and warm us in the winter months. Fostering a sacred attitude for the wood we use is part of the caretaker's attitude. The caretaker knows that wood is made of sunlight, water, wind and air. Wood is the future homes for all sorts of creatures and the soils of Earth in the future once it has decayed.

When looking at a standing dead tree, you might think it would be perfect for firewood. Taking a longer-range view, you see it as a home for various animals and insects and as a food source for birds. Anytime you take something like wood out of the equation of future life, it is good to do it in a respectful, caring manner.

When collecting wood, either dead or living, I look for places where harvesting the wood will make the environment healthier. I once came upon two red maple trees growing close together, rubbing against each other's trunk when the wind blew. The rubbing action was creating abrasions in both trees, and they were getting diseased. I knew that if one tree was gone, the other would heal and flourish, so I had to choose which tree I should cut down.

You might ask if that isn't like playing God? Well, yes, it is, and someone has to do it. Humans have a unique responsibility as caretakers and gardeners to contribute to a balanced ecosystem. Like the wolf who keeps deer populations from overgrazing vegetation, like the coyote who keeps rodents in check, humans have the ability to view an ecosystem as a whole and choose to move a system toward balance.

Remember, survivalists are tools of the Creator. Whatever they touch is a healing to the Earth. It is an action to reduce struggle and create healthier spaces. In some places a more aggressive approach is needed. When one species of plant is invading an ecosystem, destroying its balance and crowding out the diversity of the area, major action is called for to remove the invasive species.

Our body is our primary shelter, our first line of protection from the elements. Through our body and all of our senses, we receive a constant flow of information from the environment. Viewing indigenous peoples throughout the world, you notice that many of them go about mostly naked with much of their skin exposed to the elements. Instead of being primitive or "backward," which Europeans labeled indigenous peoples because they didn't clothe themselves like they did or use the tools and inventions that made the settlers lives more comfortable, the native dwellers embraced their surroundings, moving within the cycles of the seasons. They exposed areas of skin so that they could feel and interact with all around them. Their skin felt the subtle changes in the wind. At the same time, their ears were attuned to the symphony of sounds around them; their noses were highly sensitive to the blend of smells in their environment; their eyes scanned near and far, picking up the tracks and sign left by animals or other humans.

The Indians used flint and obsidian while the Europeans had iron and steel. Europeans wore multiple layers of clothing and rarely bathed. As a result, Indians could smell them coming from a long distance away. Indians constantly bathed themselves in the rivers and lakes regardless of the season. They purified themselves in sweat lodges and as a way to de-scent themselves before undertaking a hunt.

Indigenous peoples are anything but backward. To them, the Europeans who pushed their way onto their lands were the backward ones who had no idea how to live with the Earth, constantly in a struggle against the natural order. The Native Americans chose to live close to the Earth, and they saw themselves as one with everything around them. When they had celebrations and ceremony, these "backward" people dressed in beautifully crafted clothing with designs that had personal meaning to them. They wore finely tanned buckskins or animal pelts and colorful cloth woven on primitive looms, all decorated with intricate beadwork limited only by their imagination.

Think about how to define what shelter really is, what that word stands for. Generally, the answer is that shelter is a place where we are protected from the elements, regardless of the season. Grandfather taught us to see ourselves, our bodies, as our most important shelter. The bottom line in survival is to protect yourself, as well as anyone else who is with you. In order to protect yourself, you have to know when you are in any kind of danger, from the elements, from heat and cold, from contaminated water or from predators in the area. Grandfather showed us we could use our bodies to feel and know what was going on around us. We first learned how we experienced that feeling of danger in our gut, a visceral response to what was happening around us. He led us to a place deep inside, where our instincts lay, a place where the visceral feelings that emerged had many applications. This inner place of feeling, once developed, became a tool for self-reflection, a place that warned us of oncoming danger, a place of communication with the world around us and much more.

Grandfather combined these lessons with what he called the Prayer of Early Warning and Danger. He said that each morning and each evening in our sacred sit area, we should add to our devotions a prayer, asking the Creator to send us a warning of any oncoming danger. So if danger was approaching us, or any of our family members or loved ones, we would get a feeling that something wasn't quite right, and through surrendering to the feeling, we would know not only what that danger was but we'd also know where that danger was coming from. This prayer has alerted me to danger countless times in my life.

Grandfather told us that when we surrendered, we should let go of all thought, all emotion, time and expectations, all of our past and any future or destination. He taught us to then pay attention to the first sign, symbol, word or phrase that came into our minds.

An example of how the Prayer of Early Warning and Danger came in handy happened when I was driving with my mother. I began to feel strongly that something was not right as we approached a stoplight about two blocks in front of us. I couldn't just say to my mother to pull over because I had an uneasy feeling, so I told her I was feeling sick and was going to throw up. I urgently asked her to pull over. After we pulled over, I opened the car door as if I was going the throw up, and then I leaned back into the car, telling my mother I felt better. And I did feel better although the uneasy feeling was not totally gone, but it was weaker. My mother pulled back into traffic, and the car that had been behind us was going through the stoplight ahead of us. All of a sudden, a garbage truck blew through the red light to our left and clipped the back end of the car in front of us while we were still a half a block away. My mother gave me a funny look, somehow knowing my protestations of feeling sick and wanting to pull over had been tied to our not having been slammed into by the garbage truck.

Grandfather linked the Prayer of Early Warning and Danger to the place of instinct deep inside of us, teaching us to trust those gut feelings we experience and opening a doorway to an inner place of knowing. The first time Grandfather revealed this awesome tool, Rick and I learned how to use it as a place of self-discovery, a place that cuts through the workings of our logical minds and helps us discover deeper levels of self-understanding.

The saying "our body is our temple" has meanings on many levels. When interacting with plants, Grandfather taught us different ways to know how a particular plant feels to us. Essentially, he showed us ways to interpret our gut reaction to asking a question about a plant. We learned how we could have a conversation with the plant and ask what its medicinal or herbal uses were, or if that particular plant was safe to eat. We also learned to ask what would make that plant or the area where it grew better thrive. These are questions he taught us to answer through sitting with plants and through surrender, learning from the plants themselves and how to interpret the signals our bodies sent to us.

In my *Guide to Wild Edible and Medicinal Plants*, I present how Grandfather encouraged me to interact with the plant world. Each plant addressed in the book has corresponding stories of my experiences learning how to identify and get to know each plant: what each plant's unique properties are and how/when to harvest and prepare them. Grandfather had what I have come to know as a unique way of discovering the properties of any plant species. He taught us how to know whether the plant was edible and/or medicinal and what types of illnesses or afflictions a plant was helpful in healing. Grandfather gave Rick and me a series of exercises aimed at teaching us ways to communicate with any plant or tree in order to discover its particular properties. First off, Grandfather guided us through these exercises designed to give us a tool to better know ourselves. These exercises had to do with using the core or center of our body, located a little below the solar plexus and deep inside one's torso, in order to connect with this place of instinct. Of course, how people experience these "places" is unique to them. Sometimes Grandfather would call this the inner place of the subconscious. The exercise he taught us had to do with connecting with those places inside of us and discovering how those inner places felt when we were in different emotional states and what those inner places felt like when they were tight or relaxed. These exercises went on over a long period of time, with us working sometimes for weeks on one particular exercise.

To help us sensitize ourselves to our inner cores, the first exercise Grandfather gave us had to do with our asking ourselves a series of questions in a specific order. He also taught us something he called "rebounding." The rebounding part of the exercise became a tool both Rick and I learned that we could apply to just about any situation or problem we needed answers to.

Grandfather had us go to our sacred sit areas to do this exercise so we could focus on this inward journey and not be distracted. Grandfather taught us to begin our sacred sit time at sunrise and sunset first connecting with what he called the Temples of Creation. That meant for us to just be in the moment, appreciating and expanding our awareness to whatever was happening in the environment around us. Grandfather said to sit in wide-angle vision, to enjoy the play of light and shadow, to listen to the birdsong and chitter of insects, all the while expanding our senses.

After a while, once we felt a connection to that particular moment in time, we were to ask ourselves from that place deep inside, "What am I feeling?" Grandfather said that when we asked ourselves this question, to ask it in a kind, gentle, loving, nurturing, mothering way—not to ask from a place of self-judgment, but from a place of self-discovery.

Once that question was asked, he said to surrender. By surrender, he meant for us to let go of all expectations, all time and history—to find a place where the past and the future did not exist. The surrender he described was not a negative surrender, like being defeated; it was a letting go, a purification. He encouraged us to clear ourselves of all emotion, to become neutral in our emotions and expectations, paying particular attention to the first thing that returned to us no matter how strange or unlikely it seemed.

Grandfather explained to us how our minds are on one hand our greatest allies and on the other hand our greatest enemies, and how people in modern society have been taught to use their logical minds to understand and judge everything they encounter. He went on to say how the education systems are based on accumulating information and regurgitating it, never teaching students to think for themselves. In modern society today, the emphasis on logical thinking has become the dominant focus, leaving our intuitive selves and minds undressed and untrained. Grandfather said our logical minds try to put every experience in its own box and to solve every problem by being in control of our perceptions. He said that through surrender, we empty our cups and are ready to receive information that is pure and undiluted. That was why he stressed paying attention to the first thing that came back from surrender. This allowed us to capture what came to us before the logical mind had a chance to jump in. How many times have you ignored the first thing that came to mind that later proved to be exactly the right response?

After we surrendered to the question, we were to focus on the first feeling that came into our minds or bodies. He told us to feel how our bodies responded to the question and what images or words returned. Grandfather also told us to note the feeling that came back from our inner places of instinct.

He said to ask, "What am I feeling?" four or seven times. Actually, if you're like me, sometimes I will ask it many times, trying to go as deep as I can when researching a question.

Both those numbers, four and seven, are sacred to the Apache. The Seven Arrows Ceremony is the focus in almost all Apache ceremonies. The number four is also sacred to them. One example is the Sacred Order of Survival: shelter, water, fire and food. Another is the cardinal directions of north, east, south and west. There are four rounds in a sweat lodge, and a vision quest is normally four days long.

Grandfather said after we had surrendered four or seven times and made a list of all the feelings that came back from "What am I feeling?" to then rebound the feelings. Rebounding is, in a sense, bouncing the word/emotion off your body, that place of instinct. Grandfather told us to read through our lists of emotions, reflecting on each word and tuning in to our core self to determine which word on the list felt "right" to us and then circling that word and leaving it out. Then we were to rebound through the list again, picking out the next word that felt right. We found that rebounding helped us get around the confines of our logical minds and opened a door to a new place inside of us. Then we went through the list again, discounting the one we circled, until we found the next word that felt right.

The first time I ever did this exercise, I surrendered to the question "What am I feeling?" four times. With my first surrender, the feeling of being happy came to me. I thought to myself that of course

I was happy. There I was, with my two best friends in the world, experiencing a new way of living close to the Earth, learning so much and living my dream.

The second time I surrendered to what I was feeling, the feeling of fear came back. This really threw me. I had no idea where that feeling was coming from, but I noted it because it felt so right. Grandfather had warned us not to question what came back, but to note it and move on.

On the fourth surrender, the word that came to me was "apprehension." Again, I remembered feeling puzzled with that word/feeling, but again let go of my judgment and noted it because it also felt right to me for a yet unidentified reason.

When I did the rebounding part of the exercise, the first word that felt right to me was "fear." *OK*, I thought, *whatever.* I had no idea why and kept going. Apprehension was the other feeling that felt right to me.

The next stage of the exercise Grandfather had laid out was for us to ask ourselves, "Why am I feeling this way?" With this part there was no rebounding; you only ask the question once and surrender deeply to that place of instinct. So I did. I took the next step. I wanted to know why I was feeling afraid and apprehensive. I had to know where these two feelings were coming from and what they meant.

This time when I surrendered, a lot of information came flooding back to me; it really surprised me how clear the answer was. I realized the fear and apprehension had to do with my fear of letting Grandfather down. I held him in such high esteem and valued his teachings so much, I was afraid that my work on the skills was not good enough, afraid that he thought I wasn't trying hard enough to absorb all the lessons he was teaching us.

Then I took the last step in the exercise. I asked the question "How can I heal this?" If the situation or feeling did not need healing, Grandfather said to ask, "What more can I learn from this?"

The response I got to my question of how I could heal that fear and apprehension again surprised me in its clarity and simplicity. What came back to me was that all I needed to do was to do my best and work hard on all the skills and lessons Grandfather had us working on. I now knew that if I was passionate in how I approached Grandfather's teachings, I would never let him down. This realization took away the pressures I'd been placing on myself, and I felt a new freedom to immerse myself in working the skills.

As I walked back into Grandfather's camp after first doing this exercise, he looked up at me and said, "I see you have met and let go of the fear you have been holding on to." At this point, he knew what I had been going through before I'd had any idea of my inner struggle.

When you are acting as a caretaker and healer in nature, there are multiple ways to use your instincts to carry out the needs or actions you are working to address. Using your gut feeling, that visceral place inside, can clue you in to whether an action feels right to you or the opposite, where a feeling of something being "not right" returns from surrender. It can be a place inside of you that helps you know what to select and what not to select from nature.

Imagine you need a number of green sticks or saplings for a particular project—say, building the frame for the door of a debris hut, where you want flexibility in the frame to weave the grid on each doorframe that holds the leaves and debris that act as the door's insulating properties.

Wandering the landscape, you are led to a clump of bushes, each struggling for sunlight and room to grow. You look through the clump of bushes and ask yourself, "Should this one be taken? Should that one be taken?" Each time you surrender and pay attention to the visceral feeling inside that connects with that place of instinct. When that feeling of release comes from the question and then surrender, you know to take that one. The caretaker wants to remove the weak, sick and diseased stalks, leaving the healthiest to have a better chance of not only surviving but thriving. Asking the question, surrendering and identifying the feeling that returns—be it a release or a tightening of your gut—guide you in what to take and what not to take.

You can use this same method in assessing an area of land that is in need of caretaking. Instead of asking the same question asked for thinning a clump of plants, you ask one for the whole area, something such as: "What plants, bushes or trees need to be removed?" or "Which plants need to be here for the betterment of the area and as food for the animals"? Again it is your inner instinct, your gut feeling and correct interpretation of that feeling, that shows you the caretaking steps that are needed to make the area stronger and healthier.

When it came to the plant world, Grandfather showed us how we could use our inner self to learn about specific plants. He had us sit for a while with a plant to observe it as a whole and in minute detail. Then he had us ask the plant, "How do you make me feel?" and surrender. Of course your questions can be more specific as well, such as asking, "What ailments are you [the plant] good for?" Whenever you ask such questions of a plant, especially at first, always research your results. Look up the plant to find out if it has any medicinal or edible properties and what they are. Then compare your "instinctual" results with what your research reveals. This procedure is not only a safety measure; each time your results coincide with what your research reveals, you build your belief system.

Grandfather also had Rick and me do this exercise with oak trees and pine trees. Little did we know that there are twenty-eight different medicinal uses from the different parts of an oak tree. It was a race to see who could discover all the medicinal uses an oak tree can provide. Of course we proved out the information we received from our questions and surrenders to the plants. We looked them up and read about their particular uses. We both had a near obsession with field guides about any natural subject, from insects to plants to amphibians and reptiles, not to mention mammals and birds. Over time, our belief systems regarding the information we received from our inner cores grew stronger as did our faith in the process.

I also believe each person's vision of who they want to be and what they stand for is a form of shelter. When times are really tough, it is who we are that gets us through it or not. For me, living my vision, constantly restating it to myself to discover the subtle ways my vision changes over time, helps me understand how I have grown and where my journey in life is moving toward. Sure there are some parts that are the same each time I review my vision, often during my morning sacred time. At the core of my vision are living my life as a child of the Earth; being a protector and healer, a warrior for the Earth; and, most important to me, sharing Grandfather's vision of passing on the physical skills and the philosophical truths he accumulated and tested out in the wilderness during his sixty years of wandering so they will not be lost.

Grandfather taught and demonstrated, through the exercises he had Rick and me do, how we are connected to what he called the Spirit That Moves In and Through All Things. This spirit connects every aspect of the world of nature. The Chinese call this energy the Force, *Chi* or *Qi,* and often Grandfather would use the Force to describe the Spirit That Moves In and Through All Things. The Force directly connects with our instincts, and we receive messages from it in the form of signs, symbols, dreams, emotions and feelings. These messages connect with our primal feelings and are the inner language of the subconscious. The main communicators we rely on when interpreting communications with the natural world are emotions and feelings. When we want to better know the properties of a particular plant, or really any natural entity, it is our feelings and emotions that at first answer questions such as: "Should I collect this? Or should I not collect that"? We ask ourselves if the return from our surrender, after asking the question, feels "right" or "not quite right."

When I am teaching students how to take these questions into the field and learn to interpret those feelings of "right" and "not quite right," seeking that feeling of release that indicates a positive response that returns from surrendering to the question, it takes my students only between twenty and thirty minutes to learn the process and begin getting results. From there they can distinguish if a plant is edible, medicinal or poisonous, or they can ask where the nearest deer is bedded down or where a certain type of plant can be found in the landscape, saving hours or even days of searching. I do this class after class, so it's not something that is in any way magical, nor does it involve any hocus-pocus. When this is done correctly, the students learn to tap into these inner places of the subconscious where their instincts reside.

Not long after Rick and I had been spending time with Grandfather, we arrived at his camp one Friday night. As we sat around the campfire, Grandfather asked each of us what our vision was. Both of us dug deep to express how we felt and what we aspired to be.

After that night, we'd have a full weekend of activities. When we were with Grandfather, we knew that each day we would have lessons in awareness and tracking, a demanding physical workout and lessons in Grandfather's Worlds of Spirit. Another hard-and-fast rule with

Grandfather was that each morning near sunrise and each evening at sunset, each of us would spend time in our separate, personal sacred areas. The inner focus and journeys at two different times of day had some subtle differences to them. In both, we would always begin embracing what Grandfather referred to as the Temples of Creation, connecting with the present baseline of our environment. We would also give thanksgiving for all the gifts from our families, the Earth and the Creator. Then we would explore our inner place of instinct to check in, asking, "What am I feeling?"

The morning sacred sit is a time to review your vision and what tasks and goals you want to accomplish that day—a time to empower a positive attitude in meeting whatever challenges the day brings. The evening sacred time is a chance to reflect on the day, to look at what has been accomplished or not, what lessons have been learned and what challenges have been overcome.

My sacred area was at the edge of a shallow pond of water about a hundred fifty feet across, surrounded by mostly cedar trees, with sphagnum moss carpeting the ground around me and onto the floor of the pond. The pond formed as the result of several streams and springs coming out of the cedar swamp and merging together.

At the end of that weekend, not long before Rick and I would have to head homeward, Grandfather asked each of us to speak what our vision was now. I was very careful to include each element of my vision that I'd said on Friday night. When it was Rick's turn, there were some things about how he saw his vision that were different from what he'd said on Friday.

I thought to myself, *Now I've got him. That wasn't what he said on Friday night.* Understand, Rick and I were as close as, if not closer than, brothers. At the same time, the competition between the two of us was intense and ongoing. The competition between us was not a rivalry, but a way for us to push each other beyond our individual limits, and we both became stronger from it. That was a good thing too because we eventually realized that together we were much more powerful than by ourselves.

After Rick had finished describing his vision, I challenged him, saying that his vision was different from what he had expressed on Friday. Before I could say more, Grandfather spoke. He said that a person's vision is always undergoing subtle changes as he or she progresses through life, even after a few days. He pointed out that as we grow and evolve, so do our visions.

Once again Grandfather spoke to us of what our purpose in life is all about—how for him, the purpose in life has four elements: peace, love, joy and purpose. He said what we feel our purpose to be directly connects to our vision. A person's vision is what becomes his or her anchor in hard times, those times we are feeling tested or experience our faith being challenged. It is from that center, where our visions are held inside of us, that we find the strength to overcome the obstacles life presents to us. Grandfather constantly encouraged us to hold fast to our vision. Holding on to one's vision is a crucial element to someone who is a caretaker and healer of the Earth.

GO ASK THE SQUIRRELS

Shelter comes in many forms and relates to all living creatures. Some shelter builders of the natural world create beautiful and intricate forms that are highly functional. Humans, plants, forests, animals, birds, insects and some fish create different forms of shelter, often working together to do so.

Indigenous people learned the basics of shelter building from observing how different animals made their shelters. They learned the secrets of dead-air space from the squirrels and mice. They learned how, during storms, a dome-shaped shelter would be stable and dry inside, how a dome structure is structurally sound and sheds water. It was literally a matter of life and death for these people that their shelters kept them warm and dry in all weather conditions, so they used only what consistently worked in the environment where they lived.

When Grandfather Stalking Wolf told Rick and me our parents had given permission for us to spend the long Thanksgiving holiday weekend camping with him, we couldn't believe our good fortune. We had gotten into a daily routine of traveling into the Pines whenever we could to meet with Grandfather, but this was the first time we'd been allowed to overnight at his camp.

We had been preparing to leave camp for home when he told us we were going to be camping with him. The sun hung above the cedar trees toward the western horizon, and the breezes of the day were dying down when he gave us the news. Grandfather pointed out that shelter was the first need to address in any survival situation, so he said we'd better get started preparing one for the night ahead. In late November, temperatures in the Pine Barrens can drop quite a bit at night, so we got right to work. As Rick and I gleefully smiled at each other, barely able to contain out excitement, Grandfather, as he so often did, seemed to disappear into the scrub oak and pines that surrounded us. When we looked back to where he'd been standing, there was only empty space.

Since we'd never built a shelter before, our first idea was to build a lean-to. We'd used them on campgrounds before and felt a good roof would keep us dry, so we began to collect sticks and armfuls of debris. Lashing a tree limb between two pine trees, we leaned the longer sticks against the cross pole at an angle, crosshatched them with branches and covered the roof with debris. We built side walls, but had a hard time covering them with debris. We put about four inches of debris on the lean-to and then stuffed more debris inside the shelter. We built a fire about ten feet in front of the lean-to and crawled into the pile of leaves and pine needles. Both of us were looking forward to our first night sleeping in the Pines with Grandfather camping nearby.

We slept only a brief time, awaking cold and uncomfortable. For a while we alternated warming by the fire and then trying to get some sleep, but it wasn't working very well. About one in the morning, we moved the fire closer to the lean-to, and that helped some, but we were not warm, and any sleep we did have didn't last for much more than an hour at a time, if that.

When we got out of the shelter in the morning, we were covered with dew. So now we were wet and cold. As we built up our fire, we discussed how the prospect of spending three more nights like this did not appeal to either of us. Our one consolation was the fact that we had built our lean-to facing the east. As the sun rose above the horizon, its rays warmed us and worked to dry out the shelter.

Grandfather appeared at our shelter and gave us a look that said, "What happened here? This is a shelter?" Then he asked us if we had ever watched the squirrels build their shelters. He suggested that a thorough study of squirrel "houses" would help us understand how squirrels could stay warm and dry in any weather. He also said that we should model our shelter after our observations of the squirrels.

Throughout the morning, Rick and I searched the treetops for squirrel nests and observed squirrels adding leaves and small, flexible-looking sticks to their "houses." Some of the squirrel nests were two or three feet in circumference, much larger than the squirrel that lived there. The lesson that we took from our observations was we needed a lot more debris for our shelter. So during the afternoon, we went about gathering armfuls of debris and made a huge pile about five feet high and eight feet across. When Grandfather came by, one look told him all he needed to know. We could tell from his refusal to answer any questions related to our shelter and how he basically ignored us that we were missing something important. We got the distinct feeling that our idea of a shelter did not meet with his approval. His silence and stern look drove us crazy. We knew there was something we were missing, but we didn't know what we were doing wrong. The only comment he made to us was to again say, "Go ask the squirrels."

When it was time to retire for the night, we burrowed into the huge pile of leaves, pine needles, ferns and other materials we had found in our collecting. By pulling an armful or two of debris over our heads, we settled into our shelter. At first, we were warm, happy and snug in the pile of leaves. As evening turned into night, we began to feel too warm and began to sweat. We removed our coats and loosened our clothing to regulate the heat. We soon found the drawback of taking off our coats, as now we could feel every twig that we lay on, the debris got into our clothes and we itched at every exposed place. This was better than being too cold to sleep, but something about the experience didn't feel right. As we turned and maneuvered to find comfortable sleeping positions, we were slowly crushing down the debris pile's thickness; in turn, we were losing our bed of insulation. As a result, by the time dawn was approaching, we were too cold to sleep anymore.

We could tell Grandfather was not pleased with our progress as we sat around his fire that morning. He said to us, "You have not really learned the lesson of the squirrels. Did you really look inside their homes? Did you see how the squirrel's house is built to keep its shape?" We realized then we had to take a closer look at the inside of the nests. That meant climbing numerous trees to see exactly how the shelters

Here you can see the leaves bursting out of the nest's framework of twigs and sticks. Lots of insulation and dead-air space are the key to capturing body heat.
DAVID OTT

were constructed. As we explored the construction, we discovered the latticework of twigs that wove in and through the nest to hold the leaves in and keep them from blowing away. We saw the narrow entranceway into the shelter and the small area the squirrel curled up in surrounded by layer upon layer of insulation from the ball-shaped nest.

That afternoon, we found a dead oak tree with its branches fanning out toward the ground. We anchored several of the branches to the ground with stones and dead logs, then wove a number of limbs and branches through the dome. We then piled on about a foot of debris and did another layer of limbs and branches, then a little more debris. Next, we collected debris for inside the shelter and stuffed it full.

At about midnight, a light rain began to fall. Throughout the rest of the night, the rain came down, the water seeping through the leaves, dampening our clothes. After a while, we were lying in a pile of wet leaves. Then something really exciting happened. Even though our clothing was wet, we were still warm inside the shelter. This was a major victory for us. After we'd finished complimenting each other on our success, we drifted off to a sleep that lasted until morning.

When we emerged from our shelter the next morning, we ran to tell Grandfather of our success. As we warmed and dried ourselves off at Grandfather's fire, Rick and I excitedly told him how we'd been warm all night, even though we'd gotten wet inside the shelter. He gazed at us standing in the misty remnants of the previous night's rain, steam rising from our clothes, and remarked how being wet inside a shelter is not a good thing. As our excitement turned to shame, he also made some comment about us wetting our bed and asked if we would choose to accept that reality each time it rained.

This time Stalking Wolf was adamant. He told us we did not yet accept the wisdom of the squirrels. He said, "You still think you can improve on their methods," and then he drifted away.

After still more tree climbing and the close observation of several squirrel houses, we shared the things that stood out to each of us. Both of us had been drawn to the way the outer layers of the nest were thickly stuffed with leaves and they were all built in a roundish shape. None of the squirrel nests was wet in the center, even though they'd been through the same rain we had. This gave us an even greater appreciation of the wisdom of the squirrels.

We returned to our shelter, pulled out all the wet leaves from inside of it and put them on top of the shelter. We gathered some more brush and piled it onto the wet debris on the roof, working to shape the shelter into a dome, like we'd seen the squirrels do. The more layers of lattice sticks and debris we added, the more dead-air space we created. Later in the day, we collected more leaves that had dried during the sunny day to stuff the inside of our shelter. We were again careful to select leaves and debris that would not poke and itch as we slept. We decided the door was too big and narrowed the opening. Then we made a frame stuffed with leaves to create a door we could close after we kicked our way into the thick pile of leaves inside our little home.

That night we each had a good sleep. It didn't rain, but the temperature the next morning was 20 degrees Fahrenheit. We were surprised it had gotten that cold overnight and also marveled at how warm we had been inside the shelter, especially when we found the top leaves of our dome were frozen solid.

Stalking Wolf greeted us as we emerged from our improvised door.

Here is a good example of a debris hut being built by a student taking the Advanced Standard class. The door, which has not been completed, is a key element in trapping in body heat.
DAVID OTT

He didn't smile, but he did give us a nod of approval. We knew we had made progress in learning the wisdom of the squirrels.

Rick and I learned many valuable lessons about shelter on our first campout with Grandfather Stalking Wolf. The most important of these lessons was how insulation and dead-air space were the key to warmth. The insulation could be damp or wet, and it could be almost any sort of material as long as there was enough of it covering the shelter and it was made light and airy by layers of latticework creating the dead-air space that trapped our body heat inside the shelter and embraced us in a cocoon of warmth.

Over time we discovered that there were hundreds of natural materials that could be used for insulation: leaves, ferns, mosses, grasses, pine boughs, cattail down and grasses; even bark played a role as long as it helped provide thickness to the structure and helped form dead-air spaces around our bodies.

In the Standard class at the Tracker Wilderness and Survival School, all of my students are introduced to the most basic and most effective short-term shelter, the debris hut. In the Advanced Standard class, students build their own debris huts and spend the rest of the week sleeping in them. By doing so, they learn what is working and what is not working. If they are cold at night, the next day they will add more debris on the outside structure and stuff more debris inside to make the hut more efficient, creating more dead space to trap the warm air inside the hut.

Shelter in the natural world evolves from plants and animals, in a sense, working together. Only humankind can operate from a place of choice, for the animal and plant kingdoms, it's more a matter of instinct. Only humankind can choose, by becoming healers of the Earth, to make changes that improve the chances that animals and plants can thrive in a particular area.

IN MY WORDS

During my Advanced Standard class at the Tracker School, one of the most exciting moments was the first time I built a debris hut and slept in one. To say the least, I learned much from that experience. Even though it was in late August, the nights cooled down enough to teach me that making a large dome of debris over the frame was key in being warm and comfortable during the night. Each day I found myself making adjustments to the structure.

Although students are only required to sleep a few nights in their debris huts, I enjoyed the experience so much, I continued to sleep in it for the rest of that week and the following week during the Advanced Tracking and Awareness class. My tent turned into a storage unit.

There is a sense of inner satisfaction that comes from making your own shelter from the branches and leaves collected from the immediate environment. To give us some extra insulation from the ground, the class walked a few miles to an area of tall grasses. Each student collected a large bundle of grasses to tie together and carry back to camp, where we learned how to make grass mats for our debris huts. Even though the debris hut is packed with leaves, one's body weight crushes them down during the night. The grass mat gives the needed extra insulation from the cold ground that can rob your body of heat and make for a miserable night's sleep.

Breaking down a debris hut is a perfect way to practice caretaking. Instead of tearing down the structure and spewing all the debris and sticks around the immediate area, it's best to distribute the materials over a wide area, seeking places that could use some ground cover and making some brush piles for the mouse and vole populations to use as shelter and protection. Tom teaches Grandfather's philosophy that you always leave your camping area in better condition than when you found it. Yes, doing this takes time and effort, but it is another example of how we can act as caretakers and healers of the Earth.

I was in the class at which Tom first taught the "How am I feeling?" exercise, and to say it changed my life would be an understatement. Learning to open myself to the instinctual place inside of me revealed new worlds of understanding about my true self and the natural worlds around me. My belief and faith in what I innately knew grew exponentially with each "success" I experienced. For me, after a while, the whole process would happen in one step. Once I had surrendered four to seven times, I knew which feeling was the "right" one, why and how I could heal the situation or learn more from it came in one continuous moment of understanding.

Near the end of that week, Tom gave us an exercise to do in our personal sit area in which, after the first part, we were to stand up and ask ourselves, "Where is the place I need to go to receive a teaching I need?" We were to ask the question facing a direction and see if we experienced a release or tightening of our gut. If no release happened, we were to turn a bit and ask again, until we received that feeling of release. Then we were to ask how far away this place was. Was it close by or a hundred feet away? And so on until we got that release. Then we were to find the place and surrender and see what was revealed.

My sit spot was by the cedar stream that runs out of camp. I'd been using that spot for several years, and right next to where I sat, someone had left a short scout lance that stood there the whole time I'd been using that particular sit spot. It was a warm, sunny day with light breezes passing through. When I stood up to do the second part of the exercise, my gaze was immediately drawn to the opposite bank of the stream and a large patch of sphagnum moss sitting in a patch of sunlight. *No way,* I thought. *I'm not crossing the stream.* Even though I somehow knew that spot of moss was where I needed to go, I continued to turn the full 360 degrees of the circle, my gut staying tight the whole circuit. I surrendered to the inevitable and began to strip down to my underwear for the stream crossing. A close friend whose sit spot was a bit behind mine later told me how surprised he was when he looked up and saw me undressing and then entering the stream. Because the streambed was very muddy in that place, I decided to take the scout lance next to my spot to help me keep my balance and not fall in as I crossed the stream, which worked well. Once I got to the bed of sphagnum moss, the place felt so right, it was easy to surrender and to receive a personal and profound teaching. On the way back across the stream, I seemed to find a rock under the mud each step of the way, sinking to only midcalf instead of sinking to my upper thighs as I had on the first crossing. I put the scout lance back where I found it and, with a big smile on my face, walked back to camp. A month or so later, I returned to my sit spot to find the scout lance gone. Somehow that felt "right" too.

3

WATER

Grandfather often referred to water as Earth Mother's blood. When he grew up in the deserts and mountains of the border area between the United States and Mexico near the Río Bravo area and beyond, water was almost as important to Grandfather's people as shelter. His people knew that to survive they had to know intimately the sources of water. They were masters at finding water because they were so connected to the land; they experienced no separation between themselves and the environments they moved through.

To Grandfather and his people, water was a sacred entity, the way some cultures might view a goddess. Actually, all indigenous peoples, in their own ways, refer to water as Earth Mother's blood. Water is sacred; water is life, a living being to be honored, revered and protected. They view the trickling springs, the bubbling streams and the wide rivers flowing to the oceans and the oceans themselves as all being connected.

In cedar streams of all depths, Grandfather would relax his body and float with the current, letting it take him slowly along for miles at a time. Shortly after he began to take Rick and me on river floats, he

The cedar creek running through the Primitive Camp shows a profusion of lily pads, underwater grasses and clear tannin-colored water.
RANDY WALKER

taught us how we could surrender to the water while we floated. He revealed that by surrendering to the connection with that particular body of water, we could feel that body of water connecting with all other water sources on Earth. The feelings of expansiveness and deep connection we experienced from these lessons were indescribable.

When Grandfather taught us how to surrender to a body of water during our river floats, there was another side benefit that came from that surrender, one of body control. When you are immersed in cool water for any extended period of time, you lose body heat and begin to shiver. Hypothermia is a strong possibility when you are in the water for longer than a half hour, especially in some of the cool, spring-fed streams in the Pine Barrens. When you are able to fully surrender yourself to the water, your muscles do not tighten up and you don't begin to shiver. Somehow, your body relaxes into the moment, allowing you to remain immersed in the water for hours at a time. Learning to successfully maintain this form of surrender takes a bit of practice. At first, I was successful for short periods of time, but through trial and error, I soon learned how to let myself go and surrender to the water. This is one of the forms of body control Rick and I learned from Grandfather, and only after many attempts were we able to unlock the secrets of how to silence our logical minds and just be in the moment.

Cedar Creek was one of our favorite streams to float down with Grandfather. True to its name, the banks were lined with cedar trees, with tall grasses growing along parts of its banks, creating areas of sunlight and shade that we passed through as we floated along. Grandfather was always pushing us to expand our awareness, and when we were floating down a creek or river, it was no exception. That old man was always tracking, even when in the water.

There was an area along Cedar Creek where we noticed there were no whirligigs or water striders to be found. Some of the trees were dead, and the grasses at that spot were brown and stunted. Grandfather pointed this out and asked us what was happening there to cause this imbalance along the creek. Grandfather asked Rick and me to surrender to this creek bank and see what returned from that place of instinct. Rick got a taste of chemicals in his mouth. I got both the taste and smell of chemicals. My sensory experience was very strong, but there was no chemical smell in the air. When Rick and I came out of our surrenders, the air came back to smelling normal.

We then left the water at this place and explored a bit farther into the cedars. We found a tumbled-down shack that had been abandoned some years ago. Exploring further, we discovered that this shack had been used to store pesticides and other chemicals. The pesticides and chemicals had leached into the ground and made their way to the creek bank and into the water, killing the trees and vegetation at that one spot. To the untrained eye, it would just have been another twenty feet of real estate, but when you looked closer, it went from healthy vegetation to dead vegetation or plants that were struggling to grow up or dying. Then, as you moved down the creek, the vegetation slowly got better and better until it was back to normal health. So that section strongly indicated something had happened on that bank of the creek.

When you see these small insects moving on top of a body of fresh water, dancing this way and that, marking their territory by chasing away intruders, you know that the water is not polluted. That doesn't mean it is perfectly safe to drink, because of parasites, but if you boiled it for a while or had a really good water filter, you could drink the water or cook with it. Those water insects are an indicator, and when you don't see them, it's a sure sign the water is polluted.

Humor me in this next section and open yourself to the creation and formation of a drop of water. By taking this journey in your mind, you may get some idea of why I find it so hard to describe how all waters are connected. Let go of all preconceptions, all expectations and all your past as you participate in the imaginary journey of a drop of water. Clear your mind, take a deep breath and surrender to following along with the journey.

Imagine you are water in the ocean, rising and falling with the swells of the waves. As the sun heats the water, you find yourself leaving the body of water as you evaporate, moving into the air and feeling yourself slowly rising into the sky with the warm air. As you rise, you feel the shifts of the winds pushing you this way and that. You are rising higher and higher, surrounded by other molecules of water in the air, along with the dust and the smoke particles around you. Bumping into a particular dust particle, you join other molecules of water that have condensed on that piece of dust or ash, growing in size as warm air pushes you skyward.

Now you feel yourself slowing down as you meet cooler air. You feel the identity and energy you defined as yourself joining larger and larger groupings, rapidly becoming a tall cloud, rising and expanding, gaining speed as it grows in size, capturing more and more of the eastward-moving wind.

Inside the cloud, more and more water molecules arrive, and the

A building thunderstorm cloud rises high above the landscape.
RANDY WALKER

cloud is growing all the time. The cloud continues building in size until it has formed a towering thundercloud. Cooler air begins to move under you as strong winds move through the cloud, sometimes swirling into circular, spinning forms that push the small water and dust particles to the edges, where they bump into other water particles and grow in size.

As your droplet grows, a feeling of heaviness comes with it. The feeling is familiar. You are becoming a drop of water. You feel yourself reach that place of critical mass as you are released from the cloud. Now you are falling, gaining speed, going wherever the winds take you on your journey. You sense many other drops falling with you toward a pulling sensation that comes from the Earth.

Suddenly, you splash down on a large leaf, slide to the edge of it and fall some more. You feel yourself land on the ground with many of your brother and sister drops of water. As the ground becomes saturated with water, you become a part of a tiny flow with other raindrops and eventually feel yourself slip down a steep bank into a flowing stream. That feeling of something familiar continues to grow in you.

After twists and turns, slowing down at times while you circle in quieter waters, you feel yourself merge with a much wider, deeper river and join its motion. After a while you feel yourself growing even more as the river widens and deepens. Now there are fewer slow places; the river's flow has a strength and a power to it that feel unstoppable.

As the feeling of returning home grows stronger, you give yourself fully to the journey, moving, flowing, merging with all the other drops of water, which are no longer drops of water, joining the river.

After what could be weeks or months, you flow into an ocean. There is a subtle difference to the feeling of the ocean; it is that feeling of being home. You feel complete.

Now imagine the immensity of the oceans, the long rivers over the lands and the actions of mountain streams flowing all over the world. Then add in every other form of water, the clouds in the sky and the mists and the fogs, all happening at the same time. Now open yourself to feeling connected to all the waters on the Earth.

The average adult body's water content averages between 57 percent and 60 percent. The high range is 65 percent, and the low end is around 50 percent. So on average, more than 50 percent of our bodies are made up of water. If we don't drink any water for two and a half days, brain cells begin to die. Water is that important to us.

With the state of the Earth today, and all the challenges she faces, you might look at the situation as if Earth Mother has a form of heart disease. Waterways, large and small, are becoming clogged up in a variety of ways. Thousands of dams, the world over, have dramatically reduced the natural flow of rivers. Water is extracted from its natural systems and redirected to places hundreds, sometimes thousands, of miles away. Water is pumped to large cities to meet the ever-growing needs of the people and the industries located there. Large farming conglomerates, on immense farms encompassing thousands of acres, grow species of crops and fruit trees that demand a lot of water in order to produce well while, at the same time, communities around them are experiencing drought conditions. These farming operations also use chemicals as weed repellents and fertilizers to give their crops higher yield rates. The runoff from the chemicals is washed into streams and rivers, infecting our natural water systems, sometimes killing aquatic life and causing algae blooms. Water is like a report card for all human action; a portion of everything we do on land will run off into water. Water-quality tests can now measure in waterways the caffeine and the pharmaceuticals released from our bodies into vast water treatment plants and out into rivers. Even the water in our bodies is not separate from the world's oceans.

The water from the Colorado River is shared between nine western states. The Upper Colorado Region supplies eight states with water and the Lower Colorado Region supplies water to five states and five Indian tribes. Two of those states, Arizona and New Mexico, are also supplied by the Upper Region. The largest amount of water from the Colorado River goes to Southern California, which is allocated 27 percent of the total water usage.

There would be catastrophic effects if somehow the Colorado River became polluted or sickened by an industrial accident, or if a train derailed and spilled chemicals or oil into the river. Millions of people and their livelihoods rely on a gigantic but fragile ecosystem.

A growing reaction to corporate farming methods, and the food products they produce, has been small organic farms sprouting up all over the United States. Even the big supermarket chains have organic sections in their stores today. There has also been an incredible rise in the number of community gardens in urban, suburban and rural communities. People who work on organic farms and those who get involved with community gardens make strong connections with the Earth. They begin to tune in to the rhythms of nature, what Grandfather called "Earth Time." In Earth Time, you find yourself moving at a slower pace as you walk, your awareness expands as you observe your environment more acutely and you allow yourself to be drawn toward things that you pass in order to better appreciate that moment.

There are many people who think hard and make decisions regarding what food and chemicals they choose to put into their bodies.

Chemicals routinely found in food products made in the United States are banned in Europe and India.

Another major problem is how large-scale livestock producers use antibiotics and hormones to increase the meat production of their cattle. This has caused alarm throughout the medical community. Medical providers are increasingly concerned about the increasing number of cases in which certain forms of antibiotics are now ineffective in treating diseases and infections they routinely cured in the past. Only the high-dosage forms of antibiotics now work with certain infections, and sometimes they don't work at all. Today, a simple infection from a cut can become life-threatening. Medical researchers see a link between the overuse of antibiotics in meat production and the growing inability of antibiotics to effectively treat patients. This is one of the reasons for avoiding meat produced with antibiotics and hormones and another reason many people will only buy organic, free-range meat products.

Hydraulic fracturing, or fracking, is a major enemy of water and our water systems. Hydraulic fracturing has been found to pollute water systems and uses tremendous amounts of chemically treated water to hydro-fracture the Earth and get to sought-after gasses. One fracking operation uses millions of gallons of water to create a single well. Before the water is injected into the Earth with high-powered hoses, chemicals are mixed into the water. What chemicals they use we don't know because the various fracking companies say these chemicals are a trade secret. Environmental agencies appear powerless to investigate the short- and long-term effects to our water systems from fracking operations. As the water and chemicals are injected into the Earth, natural underground rivers, lakes and even entire aquifers are put in dire danger of becoming poisoned from the process. Naturally, the chemicals these operations use infect the soil and the rocks they pass through as well.

When hydraulic fracking is used in drilling one well, it could use between two and eight million gallons of water. To me, using that large amount of water to extract natural gas feels like a huge waste. It greatly concerns me how many chemicals are added to the water pumped into the Earth; even if the waste water from a fracking operation is reclaimed, it cannot be used again for human, plant or animal consumption.

Another form of industry that uses way too much water is our large-scale production of beef and pork products. In the raising and feeding of one steer, the amount of water required to produce one pound of boneless steak is 441 gallons, according to a UC Davis study. This form of industry is not sustainable when you consider the growing need for the potable water that eight billion people around the globe depend on. Like the organic-produce farms, organic farmers who raise smaller herds of beef cows use far less water, sometimes 75 percent less. Their animals are able to range in fields, and they are not fed chemicals to stimulate their growth or given large amounts of antibiotics to ensure their growth.

These organic farmers and the ever-growing number of community gardens show how we can meet our local food-production needs on a smaller scale and live healthier as a result. We need to address these water issues and challenges with micro and macro approaches. It's not one or the other; it's a matter of choosing to act where you are in that moment. It's seeing and acting on the opportunities you encounter to make a difference, whether it's taking garbage out of a stream or working with like-minded people to protect the water systems we still have and to be active in campaigns to clean up rivers and lakes that have become polluted.

Another focus, one that appears at first glance to be impossible to address, is how sick our oceans are from many forms of pollution and the acidification the seas are undergoing. The oil-rig disaster from the Deepwater Horizon explosion flooded the entire Gulf Coast with oil, destroying untold fish and wildlife for years to come. On top of that, the chemical agent the cleanup operations put in the ocean to break up the gigantic oil spill caused further damage to the ocean environment. Some reports have stated that the dispersal chemicals used were worse for the environment than the original oil spill.

Acidification of the ocean results from the combination of warmer ocean temperatures with acid rain. The drop of rain becomes acidified by ash particles from industrial and automotive pollution. The droplet of rain forms and then is released as acid rain. The smoke that creates these burning raindrops comes not only from industry and automobiles, but also from forest fires. With the rise in global temperatures and widespread drought conditions, forest fires are raging across the western United States and many other parts of the world. The ferocity of these fires, the number of forest fires and the size of the areas they burn are increasing each year.

Another way our oceans are in peril is from plastic products that are dumped into the ocean or washed into it by rivers. For centuries the oceans have been used as a trash can. The logic being that the oceans are so gigantic and vast, what difference could some trash thrown into it possibly make? We are now realizing that dumping that trash into the ocean can make a huge difference. Plastics, in particular, take a long time to degrade, and as a result have become a major hazard for marine life throughout the Earth's oceans.

Climate change is also playing a part in disrupting the natural currents of our oceans. The massive amounts of new cold water entering the seas from increased melting happening in the Antarctic and Arctic regions, as well as the rapid melting of the glaciers in Greenland, are changing the speed and direction of ocean currents. It was recently noted by scientists that these infusions of "new" water into the seas have begun to slow down the flow of the Gulf Stream, which brings warmer waters along the East Coast of the United States and onto the northwestern coast of Europe, flowing between Great Britain and the west coast of Europe. Without these warm waters being brought to Europe by the Gulf Stream, England and northern Europe would experience much colder temperatures, radically changing their climate for years to come. On our East Coast, large fisheries would migrate to warmer waters.

Another effect of climate change has been the changing of weather patterns around the world. In the past ten years, scientists have come up with a new term to describe climate change that is fostered by humankind's activities: Anthropogenic Climate Change or Anthropogenic Climate Disruption (ACD). These types of climate change are human induced, so it stands to reason that humans can also take the steps to reduce the activities that create these changes in the atmosphere and the oceans. Unfortunately, some scientists feel that it takes forty years for the effects of the increase in the atmosphere of carbon dioxide to reach the full range of its effects on land and sea, so if the situation we face today was created forty years ago, what will the climate look like in another forty years, based on where the planet stands today? As scary as that feels to me, I believe it is not too late to take actions to stop the roller coaster we seem to be riding down a steep and endless track, but the time for action is now, and the actions we take need to be significant, not little bit by little bit.

Anthropogenic Climate Disruption has been credited with the rising number of superstorms, which have been increasing in size and intensity. Depending on what part of the world they occur in, these tropical storms are called typhoons, cyclones or hurricanes. Hurricane Sandy was a superstorm that should have given residents of the East Coast of the United States a big wake-up call. Unfortunately, many people whose homes were destroyed by the storm are rebuilding in the same places, with the thinking that raising their home on stilts or other measures will be enough to contend with future superstorms. The death toll from Sandy was not huge, but the destruction along the shoreline from Atlantic City to New York City was huge, not to mention many residents being without power for weeks after the storm. The concerning fact is that Hurricane Sandy was losing force when it struck the East Coast, and stronger storms are predicted to hit the East Coast in the future.

In 2013, Typhoon Haiyan in the Philippines was a superstorm unofficially categorized as the strongest tropical cyclone ever observed based on wind speed. Eleven million people were affected in the Philippines, many left homeless by the storm. Haiyan's one-minute sustained wind speed was measured at 195 miles per hour when it struck.

One of the factors that contributes to the rise of superstorms is rising ocean temperatures, which cause more water to evaporate and join with storm systems. The rise in ocean temperatures is playing havoc with many ocean creatures and plants, from coral bleaching to kelp die-offs. Australia's coral reefs have been hit particularly hard, and scientists are concerned that they will never recover.

Another area that seems to be a magnet attracting superstorms is Bangladesh. In 2007, Cyclone Sidr left more than 4,100 people dead or missing. In 2008, Cyclone Nargis killed more than 140,000 people and left millions homeless. Entire villages were swept away by the storm.

Rising sea levels are another big concern with large concentrations of the Earth's population located near and on the coasts. Because of the rapid melting of glaciers and the polar regions, with more water entering the oceans than scientific models had predicted, predictive models from just a few years ago are obsolete. Now the challenge is to take the new data and create a new hypothesis of how fast and how much our oceans will rise during the next fifty years and beyond.

WHAT WE CAN DO

The causes and effects related to our fresh, potable water problems and those that the oceans face may appear to be insurmountable, but that is only if we give up hope and decide to do nothing about them. I believe if we as individuals do nothing, the consequences will be unimaginable.

I view it, as Grandfather did, from the place of a caretaker and a healer of the Earth; we can choose to act one of three ways. We can choose to do nothing, which is like burying your head in the ground or believing the numerous politicians in Washington who act and legislate like there is no problem. The second choice would be to advocate for more drilling and fracking, undermine existing environmental controls and continue to use weed-killing chemicals and genetically modified seeds and to keep giving hormones and antibiotics to farm animals, which might get them to market faster and bigger but will continue to make the problems we face worse.

The third choice is to take actions small and collective, to be aware of the environments you move through, interacting and caring for them as a caretaker and a healer of our Earth Mother. You can choose to approach caretaking from what Grandfather called the trilogy of self: physically, emotionally and spiritually. He said that when you can exist in an equal balance of your physical, emotional and spiritual selves, you can enter the Sacred Silence. In a sense, entering the

Sacred Silence is like becoming one with everything around you. You don't have to just sit there and be; you can walk in it or do caretaking while in the Sacred Silence. Eventually the place where you enter the Sacred Silence turns into the state you are always in, to one degree or another.

The premise of this book is focused on the need to make this third choice. Once you have made the choice to be a caretaker and healer of our planet, you are taking a stand for your family and loved ones, for all the trees and brother and sister plants. I see it as Grandfather would. He would plant a lance deep in the flesh of his Earth Mother and declare, "From where the sun stands in the sky, I commit my life to protecting and healing our Earth Mother and fighting against the destruction of our Earth Mother and saving all her children from the seeds of mankind's destruction."

Your vision is what drives your commitment to acting as a caretaker and healer. Everyone's vision is his or her own, just like each person has his or her own medicine. If you don't know what your medicine powers are or if you think you have an idea, the more you interact with the natural world as a caretaker, the more you will gain awareness of what your strengths are and what areas are not fully developed. Little by little, experience by experience, you will better understand how you receive communications from the natural world as you move through it.

The Spirit That Moves In and Through All Things, or the Force, connects each entity in the natural world. It is through the Force that we can communicate with the natural world, a world we are always connected to. The first step in making this connection is choosing to do so. Once we embrace the idea that everything has its own unique energy and way of expressing that energy, our connection to each aspect of nature grows. The more we experience how the Force energy is represented in all of Earth's entities and communicates messages and information, the richer our interactions with it grow. To discover the way you perceive and feel the different communications that are given to you on a constant basis, take the time to appreciate each moment. Sit with a flower blooming, sit with your back against a tree or place your hands on its bark and open your senses to that moment. The natural world is always sending us communications. It's up to each of us to become aware of and to be open to these messages.

Grandfather taught that both the Force and the spirit energy of what he called the Unseen and Eternal communicate through signs, symbols, visions, dreams, emotions and feelings. Grandfather taught that the vehicle through which you receive these communications is called Inner Vision.

Inner Vision can be a feeling or an intuitive thought. We, I believe, are always receiving communications from the world around us; the problem is, most people are blind to these communications or ignore them. Our instinctual feelings have been trained out of modern man by raising the logical mind to a high pedestal, supreme above all else.

I imagine you can relate to preparing to walk out the door on a sunny day, glancing at your raincoat as you pass it hanging by the door, but then thinking to yourself, "It's such a sunny day, I don't need my raincoat." That last thought is your logical mind jumping in. Then later in the day, as you're about to return home, the rain is coming down hard, with thunder and lightning surrounding you as you run to your car. The next time you think about your raincoat when walking out the door on a sunny day, you don't discount the thought and, instead, take your raincoat with you. Grandfather gave Rick and me many lessons to help us balance our intuitive minds with our logical minds. Modern society is heavy on logical thinking and light on intuitive feelings. Tuning in to how you receive Inner Vision and strengthening this skill helps create a balance between the logical and intuitive minds.

An important step in learning how to listen to your Inner Vision is to know yourself better and to develop an understanding of how Inner Vision communications come to you. Some people are kinesthetic; they feel more than see things. Other people are visual, and they get strong images. Sometimes the images are very clear and detailed; other times the communication can come as a fleeting image or a series of images. Kinesthetic people can learn to become very sensitive to what their body is telling them. When communicating with plants, kinesthetic people easily feel in their body just how a plant would make them feel. People with this type of medicine easily feel what state the plant is in, if it's healthy or sick or stressed.

As you build your experience interpreting Inner Vision communications that you receive, you build your belief system, success by success. Failures are also an important part of learning. Grandfather used to say that there was no such thing as failure as long as you learned from it. In understanding Inner Vision, it's also important to use your instinct as a measure as well. You can check in with yourself by asking: What am I feeling? Or how does this make me feel? Or what more can I learn from this? The questions you can ask yourself are only limited by your imagination.

There's an exercise that I have my students do, as a way to strengthen their awareness of that place of instinct, that place deep inside of you that has as many uses as your imagination can come up with. I have to add that you should never try this exercise on your own. It takes the kind of training that can only come from intensive study, not from reading this book. It's offered as an illustration of what can happen when you are properly attuned to the world around you.

I have my students begin with two cups of water: one of tap water and one of tap water that has a teaspoon of Clorox added to it. Their task is to use that place of inner instinct to determine how each glass of water—the normal tap water and the Clorox water—feels to that place of instinct. As you hold your hand over each glass of water, pay attention to how your gut feeling reacts.

Grandfather always emphasized to Rick and me, before undertaking any mission or learning exercise, for us to empower our vision, to create a need specific to the task at hand. He said that sometimes the need to learn was need enough. That is not the case when learning to connect with and feel that place of instinct in your core. To get the best results, Grandfather said we must move the need beyond ourselves, to a purpose beyond self. You might empower your vision for this exercise: "I need to learn this skill so I can protect others from drinking water that is contaminated and getting sick from doing so."

As you empower your vision, your mission to identify the safe and unsafe water, sit in wide-angle vision, your gaze relaxed, with the cups of water in the center of your vision. Then place your hand over one of the cups of water, take a deep breath, surrender all thoughts and expectations and pay attention to the first feeling or thought that returns. If your gut feels tight or something doesn't feel right, the cup probably has the Clorox water. When you feel a release in your gut, it's probably the tap water.

The learning process of connecting with the feelings and body sensations that help you identify which cup has regular water and which cup is contaminated is not easy at first; it takes practice. Even when you know which water is which, learning to connect with your place of instinct grows clearer and more distinct over time. At first, part of the challenge is being able to identify when it's your logical mind jumping in. Our logical minds are so overdeveloped, they have a hard time giving up control of the situation. That's why when taking that breath and surrendering, the first thing that you feel or think is usually from your instinct, not from your logical mind. If you can find a sympathetic partner, have him or her mix up the cups of water so you don't know which is which. Another key is recognizing when you doubt yourself. Self-doubt and distraction are two of the toughest obstacles to overcome when learning to trust and have faith in your place of instinct.

Grandfather had Rick and me do this exercise for weeks at a time. Then he had us vary how much Clorox or cleaning agent was put into the clay bowls we used, until we were using up to eight different bowls of water. One bowl of unadulterated water and the other seven bowls with different levels of contaminant chemicals added in. Then one of us would mix up the bowls, and the other would have to determine the order from the regular water to the bowl that was most polluted. The more you practice these types of exercises, the more refined those subtle inner feelings of your instinct become and the more confidence you gain in trusting your instinctual feelings.

With rivers and streams, the healthiest state for them to be in is in a state of flow. The more consistent the flow, the better for all living things associated with that particular ecosystem. The plants, fish, animals and so on—all benefit when the water flows in a regular pattern. When the waterway is not blocked, fish can swim upstream to spawn. When fish are blocked from reaching their annual spawning grounds, that particular family of a fish species is threatened with extinction unless it can adapt or people work to create water channels for the fish to use. Here is another way humankind is able to do for the Earth what she cannot do for herself.

In modern man's attempts to control the environment and harness the power of its waters, the practice of building dams has been used for thousands of years. Unfortunately, the consequences of blocking off a river's natural flow becomes secondary to the intent of why a dam was built. Along with blocking a water system's natural flow, bigger dams flood large tracts of land behind them, often relocating entire communities, sometimes flooding areas held sacred by indigenous tribes and destroying entire ecosystems. These testaments to man's "ingenuity" collide head-on with the natural order of an area.

If you live near a stream, river or lake, there are simple steps you can take to caretake the area and improve the body of water. You can commit yourself to caretaking one section of the stream or body of water, taking out any trash or discarded items and removing fallen branches or concentrations of brush and leaves that are clogging a section. If a stream or a riverbank is being eroded, trees, shrubs and ground cover can be planted on the bank to help limit erosion. It is best to use native species when possible. A little research about plants and trees that have fibrous root systems and that penetrate the soil in your area will help you decide what the best options are for plants to use. Since many fish feed on insects, some of which spend a portion of their lives on shore, planting specific native plants that the insects feed on and lay their eggs on will also benefit the fish populations as well.

Adopting the corner of a lake is also a way to start the healing process. Again it's a matter of removing debris and any silt buildups. If there are invasive species of plants crowding out the diversity of the area, removing as many of the invasive species as you can will help the area regain its biodiversity.

Remember that whatever is running off the land is going into the body of water. Pet poop that is concentrated in one area, if not cleaned up, pollutes the water for human consumption, so even if there is no law requiring pet owners to clean up after their pets, it's the right thing to do.

The streams in the Pine Barrens produce some of the finest, cleanest water in the United States, as the Pine Barrens sit over one of the largest aquifers in the country due to the sandy soils that allow rainwater to penetrate to the aquifer. The sandy soils, the lush, grassy beds inside the streams and the many small pebbles naturally filter that water as it flows through the swamps. Natural springs bubble up to join the water making its way through the streams of the cedar swamps.

Grandfather was such a connoisseur of the water from the streams in the Pine Barrens, he could tell by tasting a cup of water exactly where that water had been collected from. Rick and I were always in awe of his ability to do this. We used to try to fool him, sometimes collecting the water from two different streams. Grandfather would correctly see through our trick, naming not only both the streams where the water had come from, but also what parts of the streams. This is just one more example of that old man's awareness and passion. For him to have been that sensitive to his sense of taste and to have paid that much attention every time he took a drink of water spoke volumes.

Last fall I ran a Caretaking class at the Tracker School with more than seventy students in attendance. During the week, the students participated in a stream-healing project. The stream that runs through camp had barely been flowing; the grasses growing under the water showed hardly any movement as the flow of the water became sluggish. The stream had not been cleared of built-up silt for a number of years; fallen trees and branches clogged parts of the stream. The stream needed major help for it to regain natural flow.

The students all had sit spots along the river for this class, and they did exercises during the week aimed at discovering what the stream needed to regain its flow. Each student individually assessed what they felt needed to happen.

With a rainstorm predicted for that Wednesday night, we had the opportunity to act. On Wednesday afternoon, from the departure point of their sit spots, the students entered the stream and spent the afternoon working individually and together to implement the ideas they had formulated during the week.

The channel in the center of the stream was cleared of silt with rakes and shovels. Large branches were dragged out of the stream and a fallen fifty-foot cedar tree was cut up and moved out of the water. Places where smaller streams fed into the stream's flow were reopened by removing built-up silt so their flow was freed. Much of the muck pushed to the sides was shoveled onto the banks, building them up in places.

The ideas the individual students had come up with in their assessments were very similar for each section of the stream. Everyone was in the water, working together when many hands were needed. About three hundred yards of the stream were opened up. That night we had thunderstorms and heavy rain. After the students had finished Wednesday evening, there was a noticeable increase in the stream's flow. After the rains that night, the flow was even stronger and healthier.

This is an example of what a dedicated group of people can do. By committing yourself to a section of a stream, it will take longer to complete the project, but with consistent efforts, over a period of time, the same type of results can be achieved.

When working to free the flow of a stream or river, removing all the logs and branches can be counterproductive. Fallen logs and branches can provide complexity and pools for fish to rest and shade, and they can enhance insect life, so it's important to assess each situation independently, asking yourself if your actions contribute to the waterway's health as well as to the aquatic life that inhabits that particular ecosystem.

If you live in a house, look at the house from the point of view of rain runoff. Where does the water go? Most people don't know what happens to rainwater after it comes off the roof or out of the gutters. Whatever water is running off the land is going into a body of water, either aboveground or underground. If you find places the water runoff gets blocked, it's a healing act to remove the blockage. Sometimes a small change, like building up a slope on the land, can act as a way to trap water that is then used for gardening. Another way to help the flow is to put in small filters to trap garbage and keep it from getting into a stream or river. Always think small before you begin to think bigger. Often it's the little things that help in the immediate situation.

If you live in a dry or desert area, like Texas, the ground is hard and the rain runs right off, never penetrating the Earth. When strong storms occur, all the rainwater is quickly channeled into dry stream-beds, and flash floods can occur. To capture the rainwater where the ground is hard, punch holes in the ground about four to six inches deep. Use either a grid pattern or a pattern that is created by the lay of the land itself. These holes will allow the rain to penetrate into the ground, rejuvenating the land.

Water conservation is a given when the goal is to preserve potable water. A leaky faucet just dripping for a year can waste over three thousand gallons of water, so fixing water leaks and running toilets is a vital conservation action. Taking shorter showers has a positive long-term effect. If you turn off the water while soaping the dishes when cleaning up after a meal, then rinse off the dishes all together, you dramatically cut down the amount of water used. Any way you can stop the waste of water makes a positive impact toward preserving this life-giving resource.

Grandfather always approached water with reverence and appreciation and in a sacred manner. He saw Earth Mother's blood enriching each living entity and honored her with each step he took. Deepening your connection and appreciation for water builds greater sensitivity within you. Actions you take to preserve and protect water sources then come from your heart and feel effortless because those actions produce positive results.

Clean water is one the most important resources provided by the Earth. All life depends on water for survival. Anything a person can do to protect this crucial resource makes a positive step as a caretaker and healer, be it limiting water usage, cleaning clogged streams or plantings on riverbanks to limit erosion; each act is beneficial. Remember, even the simplest act of taking a piece of garbage out of a stream or off its banks makes a difference. It is an affirmation of caring.

4

FIRE

Grandfather often referred to the sun as "the big fire in the sky." He believed there was a direct relationship between the fires on the sun and the fires of Earth—those fires that we control and use on Earth and those fires the Earth holds herself. From the magma deep in the Earth, that one day will flow down the sides of a volcano, to the fires started by lightning—Grandfather believed both were related, both from the same source, the sun.

American Indians and indigenous peoples around the globe see fire as a sacred entity. They view fire as a powerful gift from the Creator with a definite link between the sun in the sky and the sun at our feet, in our firepits or deep in the bowels of the Earth. Still, to this day, you will find fire represented in our churches, cathedrals and synagogues by the ways candles and incense are used. The openings of many different forms of worship begin with the lighting of candles on the altar or sanctuary. Votive candles for prayers and the healing of loved ones and friends are lit in many houses of worship and homes. There's always something where fire ties us to our primal past and our present day.

Formed by beginning with small twigs, building in size, layer by layer, the triangular shape of a tepee fire will catch fire quickly and burn evenly.
RANDY WALKER

Indigenous peoples gravitate to using small fires, fires just big enough to do a specific job. Fires are used for so many things: light, cooking, water purification, toolmaking, hardening projectile points, smoking hides and fish and meat, firing pottery, making medicinal remedies and, of course, warmth.

Our ancient ancestors also used fire for protection, to ward off predators in the night as a defensive tool or to drive game toward hunting parties, off cliffs or into dead ends. Fire was used as a defense and in a proactive way. Even today, sitting around a fire at night takes us back to our primal roots. I sometimes jokingly refer to a campfire as "caveman TV."

Fire is that one element that brought us out of the darkness and into the light. Fire is sacred to the people who live close to the Earth. They never take fire for granted because they have a deep appreciation for all the benefits fire brings to their lives.

Fire has always been used as a great purifier—from boiling water to make it potable to burning rotted things that could contain disease rather than composting them. Fire has also been used in many parts of the world to send the physical body of the dead on their journey to the world of spirits. The funeral pyre has been used throughout the history of humankind. The Ganges River in India has carried the ashes of millions of people on their final journeys to the sea.

Grandfather's people held a ceremony for a clan member who had passed on. The ceremony involved burning not only the person, but his shelter and all his possessions, and the fire keeper kept the fire burning for four days. At the end of the ceremony, the ashes were scattered to the four directions and then a celebration of the departed's life was held.

Cultures from all over the world also use forms of sacred fires when holding ceremonies and rites of passage. Each tribe or clan would have one or several sacred fire keepers. The role of the sacred fire keeper was to tend the fire and to keep it burning throughout a ceremony, for days at a time when called for. The fire keeper would build the fire or direct the building of the fire, making sure each stick was placed on the fire structure in the appropriate place and manner. The fire keeper would tend the fire in a sacred, respectful manner, appreciating the role and the life of each particular fire. Ceremonial fires were just that: a fire directly connected to the ceremony.

The fire keeper was the guardian of the fire who made sure the fire was used for nothing else, no burning of trash or cooking. For the sacred fire keeper during a ceremonial fire, it was a time of quiet reflection, introspection, sometimes journeying within. They would not become distracted by idle conversation or questions from others. In some cases, especially in ancient times, the sacred fire keeper made sure the fire always burned or preserved burning coals during migrations. This way, any family whose fire went out could go to the fire keeper and get coals for their cooking and heating fires.

The sweat lodge is common to many American Indian tribes and indigenous people all over the world. Here fire is used to heat dense or volcanic rocks, the bones of Earth Mother. The white- or red-hot stones are then taken into Earth Mother's Womb, the cradle in the center of the lodge. The person running the ceremony pours water over the heated rocks, filling the lodge with steam and heat as prayers are offered and sacred songs sung.

One of the main reasons for entering a sweat lodge is purification. The purification the participants seek can come in many forms. Hunters, often before a hunt, will use the sweat lodge for purification and prayer. The hunters pray for a successful hunt—a hunt that will bring needed food to the clan or tribe. Further, they would commit themselves to show respect to the hunted animals. They promised to use every part of the animals they were hunting, letting nothing go to waste. The sweat lodge also cleansed their bodies and removed their scents.

Many tribes use the sweat lodge as a means of connecting with the spirit world, praying for guidance, conducting healing ceremonies or seeking answers to questions. Before people undertake vision quests, they purify themselves in the sweat lodge. Then they set out for places on hills called questing circles. During the Sun Dance, each morning before the dancers enter the sacred circle to begin their journeys around the sacred tree, they enter the sweat lodge to purify not only their bodies, but their purposes and visions, offering themselves and their physical and spiritual suffering for the betterment of the tribe.

There are numerous variations to use when making a sweat lodge structure. Here is an example of a Spiral Lodge, where the poles going around the lodge begin to the left of the door, connecting with the Earth and spiraling in a clockwise motion, winding to the top.
RANDY WALKER

Whenever Grandfather was going to initiate Rick and me into a higher level of spiritual teaching, we had a special place, near the swim area, we called the Waters of Joy. There we would build and enter the sweat lodge. Oftentimes, the teaching would be conveyed to us while in the sweat lodge; when the lodge was over, we would wander the landscape and begin to put to use the teaching conveyed in the lodge.

Smudging is another form of purification. Herbs such as sweetgrass, sage, tobacco and cedar are burned over hot coals and placed in a primitive shelter. The smoke drives out insects and is spiritually cleansing. Smudging is practiced in more than fifty countries, where the herbs and plants used differ depending on environment and tradition. In studies over the past ten years, it has been proven that smudging also has health benefits because it purifies the air of harmful bacteria in enclosed spaces.

Here is a quote from the 2007 study published in the *Journal of Ethnopharmacology*: "We have observed that 1 hour treatment of medicinal smoke emanated by burning wood and a mixture of odoriferous and medicinal herbs (havan sámagri which is a material used in oblation to fire all over India), on aerial bacterial population caused over 94% reduction of bacterial counts by 60 minutes and the ability of the smoke to purify or disinfect the air and to make the environment cleaner was maintained up to 24 hours in the closed room." So not only are the creepy crawlies that inhabit primitive shelters forced out by the smudging of the shelter, but the aerial organisms that could sicken us are drastically reduced by the process.

Even though there are people who dismiss medicinal smoke or smudging as a way to bring in positive energy, to call in beneficial spiritual entities or to cleanse the energies and help purify a shelter or house, the scientific studies where harmful aerial bacteria are dramatically reduced by burning certain plants give hard evidence in support of this ancient practice occurring over five continents.

In the philosophy classes at the Tracker School, I teach the different applications of smudging that Rick and I learned from Grandfather. Before entering a sweat lodge or before a ceremony is begun, all the participants are smudged. Whether you are smudging a person, a house or a primitive shelter, it is always done in a clockwise manner. If a house is being smudged, the process is begun in the basement or the lowest floor, moving room by room toward the upper story. As you move in a clockwise direction through each room, the collected negative energy is driven upward, so it is important to give that energy a place to leave the house by opening a window in the last room you will be smudging.

Bear, an early instructor at the Tracker School and a Coyote Thunder member, used to teach smudging to the students in the

Philosophy I class. Bear used his personal experience to demonstrate an important point. The story was about how one time Bear smudged his house and forgot to open a window in the upper floor—in this case, the attic. As Bear was smudging the stairs, about to walk through the door to the attic, a window at one end of the attic actually blew out of the window frame.

That's an extreme example, but a clear illustration of the need to provide an escape route for any negative energy that has accumulated in the house. The clockwise motion through the house pushes unwelcome energies in front of you as you smudge the house. Bear was letting us know that leaving an escape route for the negative energies was essential.

Indigenous people know that the wood we burn in our fires is much more than a piece of firewood. They view the wood they burn as a combination of solid sunshine, rainwater and air. Trees and plants are the future soils of life. As the wood decays, it not only provides fresh nutrients to our soils, but is used by animals and insects as their homes and shelters.

Before steel was brought to this continent, wood had to be split or broken up using rocks, stone hammers and wedges. Then firewood would have to be hauled back to a camp. Since an important principle when living with the Earth is the conservation of energy, the amount of work involved in collecting firewood made it a valued resource, one not to be squandered. As a result, the fires used by indigenous peoples were generally small, just big enough to get the job done. Small fires are easily assimilated back into the landscape by nature herself, turning those carbons into oxygen.

Whenever Grandfather, Rick and I would come upon an abandoned firepit in our wanderings, we would work as a team to return the firepit area to the Earth. This would prevent future fires being built in that spot by partygoers who come for the sense of isolation the Pine Barrens provides.

First, we would break up any chunks of charcoal into a powder form. Then we spread the ashes and charcoal in a large area around the firepit, returning nutrients to the Earth. If there was a ring of stones around the pit, we would scatter them. Then we would fill in the firepit with Earth and debris, masking all evidence that the firepit had been there.

Humankind's incessant lust to control the environment for progress and profit has led to the cutting down of almost all our old-growth forests and the disappearance of many of our woodlands. So much forestland is being destroyed, it is estimated that 1.5 acres of forest are cut down every second. I always stress to my students how when an area of forestland is taken away, not only the trees are gone. Gone too are the food and the habitats for the birds and the animals that rely on the forest. The undergrowth, without the protection of the trees, is also decimated. The streams and waterways dry up, and the carrying capacity of the area mostly disappears as well.

Planting trees in a previously cut area cannot bring back the variety of plants and bushes that coexisted with the forest unless someone helps bring those plants there. This is where the healer of the Earth comes into play, doing for the Earth what she cannot do for herself.

Through research and observation we determine what types of biodiversity work well in that particular ecosystem. Caretaking plants from a healthy area of forest and replanting them, along with planting gathered seeds beneath the young, replanted trees, will begin the process of reestablishing a healthy forest where animals and birds come to find refuge and food. The animals are driven away to seek new areas of biodiversity where they can find food and shelter. With the shrinking availability of forestland, the birds and animals are further stressed, as they must wander and migrate to find suitable wilderness areas in which to survive.

When a natural gas or oil pipeline is built, a hundred-foot width of land is cleared to accommodate its construction. Whatever ecosystem is in its path is disrupted. When a leak or a spill occurs, real damage is done, and it can take generations for that place on the landscape to heal. The animals, birds and fish killed by the original spill are gone. The waters of streams and rivers become polluted and often the "cleanup" and chemicals used to disperse the spill are more harmful to the ecosystem involved than the original spill.

This brings up the questions many people are trying hard to find answers to: Are the peoples of the world going to continue burning fossil fuels? Or can other forms of energy that provide our energy needs without destroying and degrading the Earth—its air, waterways and oceans—be employed? How long will it be until the negative effects of humankind on our Earth Mother's ecosystems render entire regions uninhabitable?

Sometimes it feels that it's already too late, that we've gone too far. I, for one, refuse to give up hope and continue to hold on to my vision of working together and individually as healers of the Earth. Those who choose to will begin what in the future will be the norm: reclaiming natural areas and ensuring their balance so our grandchildren's grandchildren will be able to experience the joy, wonder and sense of connection with the natural worlds around them.

It seems that for many people, in winter or summer, anything warmer or cooler than 75 degrees Fahrenheit is a sin. Most of the time, we, as with everything else, deal in excess.

Our fires are too big, so to speak. We send massive amounts of pollutants into the air with our big fires. The big fires I'm referring to have to do with the volume of scale of what we burn today in our cars, trucks, industrial uses and coal, natural gas and nuclear power plants. All heating and air-conditioning units need energy to operate. All the energy going into the packaging of products, not to mention what it takes to manufacture the products, affects our air, water and land. All of these things rely on fire—that one element that brought us out of the darkness and into the light. The misuse of our resources is a major factor in what is wrong with the Earth today. The question becomes: "How can we live our lives in ways that limit our uses and abuses of the energy footprint of just about everything we use and consume in our everyday lives?" Even the wrapper of a candy bar probably uses as much energy or more than the making of the candy bar itself.

We've totally mismanaged our fires to the point of nearly destroying the Earth. Because of all the mitigating factors we have brought about, we have caused damage in one form or another to practically everything modern man has touched. For far too long we have been wasteful, using resources that cannot be replaced. In doing so, we've polluted the very Earth, changed its natural cycles and set in motion the extinction of numerous species of animals, fish, coral reefs and plant life. In the desperate attempt to capture the energy of the sun, we have provided nearly our own destruction and the destruction of the planet.

GRANDFATHER AND THE SACRED TEMPLE OF FIRE

One of the most inspirational and spiritual things I ever saw Grandfather doing happened late one night. I was on the way to Grandfather's camp, and it was one of those nights when it was absolutely overcast and pitch-black. The woods were thick with mist. I could barely see the narrow deer trail I was following. The only reason I could see anything at all was because I was using extreme wide-angle vision. Back then you couldn't see any city lights at all, even from the tops of the hills. I was heading up to his camp in this area where it had been burned several years before, and the scrub oak bushes were about chin to head high and very, very thick.

I was still a ways from his camp, when all of a sudden I noticed this glow deep in the scrub oak bushes. The glow would expand, taking on a yellowish-orange color and, after a moment, diminish to an orangish glow. The glowing place looked like something breathing. I felt confused and thought I was seeing things. My first thought was it was an aura, or spirit; my imagination was running wild in that moment. I watched this glow expand and contract; it would glow and diminish, then glow and diminish again. Having no idea of what I was seeing, I started to feel spooked and apprehensive, so I got into a stalking mode. As I stalked closer, I realized that at times I could see a flicker of tiny flames.

As I got even closer, I could see this tiny little fire in the distance, and I could see Grandfather hunched over it, almost like a mother nurturing a child. And as I went closer still, I will always remember that moment. There was Grandfather sitting over this tiny little fire. His hands were in his lap, like he was in prayer. I could see his lips moving as he softly talked to the fire, and his body actually trembled.

The fire was barely six or seven inches big around at the base and not more than eight inches tall. It was a tepee fire with this elegant little candlelike flame, totally smokeless. Grandfather had a pile of tiny little sticks next to him, none of them any bigger or thicker than a ballpoint pen. The give-and-take of his feeding the fire, then pausing while the fire responded, was like this unbelievable form of worship. I was stunned by the beauty of it all. I was stunned by the relationship between Grandfather and the tiny little fire.

As I drew closer still, I could see even more clearly the give-and-take between Grandfather and the fire going on. Grandfather would give to the fire, and he'd seem to listen with all his senses to the fire's response. It was this elegant, beautiful, flowing breathing, almost like a pendulum, like a ceremony of worship and appreciation.

Whenever the fire would slowly die down, Grandfather would carefully feed it two or three sticks, and it would rise back up again. He'd sit there and watch it as his lips moved in prayer, his body continuing to tremble. There was an intimacy between him and the fire, like I'd never seen before; I could see him talking to the fire.

Yes, I had seen him around other big fires, sweat lodge fires, ceremonial fires and sacred fires. I had seen him talking to those fires, but not with the intimacy that I bore witness to that night.

It was then that Grandfather introduced me to what he called the Sacred Temple of Fire. I wish I could say there is only one use of that fire, the appreciation of fire, but this Sacred Temple of Fire has a multitude of uses, a laundry list. It is unbelievable how many things Grandfather used that Sacred Temple of Fire for. For the act of presence, feeling presence, sensing presence, the spiritual world, the world of the Force, the keepers of the Force—the list goes on and on and on. It was almost like this became a magic window that would transport us to a lesson that Grandfather deeply wanted us to learn and we deeply wanted to know.

A fire that small has to be taken care of frequently. He kept placing sticks on it, it kept flaring up a little bit and dying down and then he'd place more sticks on it.

I realized there was this tremendous communication going on, this tremendous intimacy. And in the blackness and the mists that surrounded Grandfather, it was like this aura of light that encompassed him. It was so exquisitely beautiful to see his lips clearly moving in prayer. That was when Grandfather explained to me the power of the Sacred Temple of Fire. Grandfather often used fire as a teacher. Fire responds to you, and there's no greater response than from a Temple Fire. When you enter that intimate give-and-take relationship with a Temple Fire, alternately feeding the fire and sitting back and embracing the fire's response, you build a powerful form of communication. Over the years, I have learned to use the Temple Fire as one of the most powerful meditations and communicators with the Creator and with creation itself.

TEACHING FIRES

In some of the philosophy classes at the Tracker School, I use an exercise that Grandfather taught Rick and me called Two Fires. The students build two medium-size tepee fires. As one fire is built, each piece of wood is empowered with appreciation, thanksgiving and prayers. The students honor the fact that they are taking this wood from future generations, because through burning it, they are taking away the soils and nutrients the wood, if it had been left to decompose on the land, would have provided.

The second fire, sometimes using wood that was broken off from the same sticks before being empowered, is built with no prayers, no appreciation, only a neutral attitude. Once the fires' structures are built, they look the same. They are the same size and shape, situated about ten feet from each other. Then both fires are lit at the same time.

The fire with the prayed-for wood and the other fire burn in totally different ways. The prayed-for fire burns bright, there is little smoke, the flame is unified in a candlelike form and, in the end, the fire collapses in on itself. The randomly built fire exhibits none of

The fire where the wood was empowered with appreciation and gratitude catches quickly and burns brightly. The fire with the wood that was not empowered, even though the same batch of wood was used to make both fire structures, is hard to get started and begins with more smoke than flame.
DAVID OTT

these characteristics. The flames are haphazard, rising up in separate groups. There is much more smoke, and when this fire burns down, it will collapse to the side, losing its cohesiveness.

The differences these two fires exhibit are so clear that we once filmed the burning of the two fires. Even on film, one can clearly see they are far different from each other. Even people who are skeptical or uninterested in a spiritual path will admit they can see a dramatic difference in the two burns.

Another exercise I've had my students do involves building three fires all the same size and with the same kinds of wood. The three groups of students building the three fires each have a different purpose in mind during the building of the fires.

Again this involves empowering the wood used to build the separate fires. Each of the fires is built with the intent of what the fire is meant to provide. The purpose of one fire is to provide light and heat, so during the building process, that is how the firewood is empowered. The intent of the second fire is for cooking, so during the building process, that is the intent that is placed in the wood and building process. The purpose of the third fire is as a utility fire, one for tool-making, fire hardening and other skills.

What these three fires are meant to demonstrate is how strong a relationship exists between the people who build the fires and how the fires will respond in return. I have my students use fire as a teaching tool and a communicator in many different ways. It is important not only to learn how to build a fire that burns well, but to learn how to build a specific relationship with a fire and experience how the fire will respond to the energy that is given unto it.

Again, when the three seemingly identical fire structures were lit at the same moment, the way they burned was unique to their identified purposes. We were later able to see on film three distinctly different burns. The fire for light and heat had a uniform burn, brighter than the other two, and it gave off powerful waves of heat. The cooking fire burned hot and then collapsed into a rich bed of hot coals, perfect for either cooking directly on the coals or placing a flat stone braced above the coals to be used as a skillet or griddle. The utility fire burned in a totally different manner. The burn of the wood was a slower, more even burn. It gave off more smoke, and its burn lasted a longer time than the other two.

Even when using a hand drill or a bow drill to start a fire, students quickly learn that there is much more to the process than the carving of the drill, the handhold and the bow. Cutting the notch in the fire-board and burning in the hole need a certain precision. Just how deep the notch is cut into the diameter of the hole being drilled can make the difference between getting a coal hot or not.

A strong sense of accomplishment and connection is felt when a person creates a coal using primitive fire-making skills. When the coal is joined with the tinder bundle and gently blown into a flame, it is as if a new life has been born. The process is much more than the mechanics involved. Before beginning to start the fire-making process, connecting with the Creator and giving thanks for the gift of fire can make all the difference. Especially when making a fire in the rain or on a cold, windy day, you find that by first honoring the gift of fire, you can get a coal and blow it into flames in the most adverse conditions.

Grandfather displayed more of his coyote teaching skills in how he introduced Rick and me to the bow drill. As we approached the camp one day, we could see Grandfather down in a crouch and doing something with his arms. As we got closer, he quickly hid behind him what he had been using. Smoking in a tinder bundle before him was a new coal, waiting to be blown into flame. Rick and I peppered Grandfather with questions. What was that thing he was holding? What was he doing? How had he gotten that coal?

Grandfather acted reluctant to tell us what he was doing or show us the bow-drill kit. Eventually, he did, but he refused to teach us how it worked. He told us we were not ready to learn this skill; we were too young, not strong enough and so on. Rick and I countered each of his arguments, telling him we were ready to learn the skill; we were old and strong enough. Grandfather finally gave in and showed us his bow-drill kit, explaining how each piece worked together, how the notch was made and the hole burned in. He then said for us to build our own kits using green oak as material.

Rick and I went right to collecting the green oak and building our kits. For much of the afternoon, we were sawing away with our bows, working to get a coal, some smoke, anything, but the results were non-existent. And those results didn't get any better over the next few weeks. Each day we spent time working on our form, recarving the spindle, making adjustments to the notch in the fireboard, to no avail. My right arm felt like it had grown twice as big as my left, like the mismatched claws of a fiddler crab. At one point, I even used my father's drill press, and even that didn't work.

Throughout this whole time, Grandfather stayed in the background, observing our progress or lack thereof. Then one day, he approached us as we bowed away and motioned for us to stop. He pointed to an old, dry, broken-off section of a cedar tree and instructed us to make kits out of that. A while later, Rick and I were both ready to try our newly made kits. In less than a minute, both of us had coals smoking under the notches of our fireboards. Our joy at making the coals was mixed with the question of why making these coals had been so easy.

Grandfather then told us he wanted us to perfect our form first so we didn't fall into any bad habits. He said using the green oak helped us do this in a big way. And then the old coyote teacher said to us, "Never use green oak," and silently vanished into the underbrush as only Grandfather could.

As we explore different ways to view fire from two perspectives—the big fire in the sky, the sun, and the fires that we have some control over on Earth—similarities between them begin to emerge. In the present day, with particulate matter in the air reaching new heights of concentration and density, individuals are changing how they use the powers of fire, discovering ways to modify how much "fire" energy they burn at home and in transportation to limit the growing effects of carbon and other chemicals in our air, soils and bodies of water.

As for the power of the sun's rays on Earth, we can't stop the sun, but we can employ behavior to make sure the sun doesn't do damage. The climate changes we are experiencing along with record temperature increases all over the globe are causing record numbers of people to make changes in their lives in order to adapt to new climate realities. From desertification due to long-term droughts, powerful storms, rising sea levels and flooding, millions upon millions of people's lives have been affected over the past ten years.

Our weather patterns are driven, in large part, by the sun. The heat of the sun drives the winds, causes water to evaporate and even affects the currents of the oceans. The best way people can have a healing impact and help address this seemingly overwhelming issue is to reduce their carbon footprints however they feel drawn to attack this issue.

If you go outside on a sunny day and you are pasty white, if you don't put on sunscreen or cover your skin, you will get sunburned. It can be the same kind of thing with certain plants. By planting shade trees and plants that will protect the undergrowth from becoming burned by strong sunlight, you can provide a sort of sunscreen for those plants. Many places on Earth are becoming parched and dry. There are some mitigating circumstances for this, but changing weather patterns can be traced right back to the sun.

As global temperatures rise, plant life and trees in temperate zones won't be able to deal with the hotter, dryer temperatures. Plants from warmer regions will slowly migrate north in the United States. Instead of waiting for the birds, winds and animal populations to bring the seeds of plants that thrive in warmer climates northward, a person can help this process happen a lot faster by planting species from warmer regions that are more heat and drought resistant in a region that's in transition. Importing plants to an area where warming temperatures and drought conditions cause die-offs in species unable to adapt to the heat and dryness helps create new forms of biodiversity. The imported plants will help keep an area green. The more green plants and trees, the more new, fresh oxygen will be released into the air and the more carbon will be absorbed by the woodlands.

Since the 1970s, people who were concerned about man-made effects to the environment due to increased carbon output have been seeking ways to lower their carbon footprints. The number of people who are concerned about this issue has increased over the past fifty years, especially in recent years as the environmental impacts that we have experienced have had a significant hand in creating habitat loss, escalating the effects on our day-to-day lives. With technology having grown by leaps and bounds, there are many more options to choose from when looking at what one person can do to help reduce the carbon footprints they leave.

What would happen if in their homes, people turned off one light that they were not using each night or two lights or even three? Imagine how much energy that could potentially save through the cumulative effects. Conscious choices about the kinds of food we eat can make big differences; by purchasing locally grown foods that are not shipped long distances to get to market, we not only eat healthier, but in most cases, we also reduce our energy footprints at the same time. By changing how we drive our cars, however good or bad their gas mileage, we can make a difference. Gas is saved by accelerating slowly and maintaining a consistent speed, relative to traffic conditions. When we brake less by anticipating the actions of the flow of traffic, less gas is needed to resume speed, and gas is saved by slowing down with just taking one's foot off the accelerator. Then, of course, there's just driving more slowly.

Grandfather taught and lived the philosophy of going without time, destination or expectation. So many people driving on the highways are in a rush to get where they're going. Those drivers blasting down the fast lane are heading someplace as quickly as they can. Grandfather always advocated moving *toward* a destination, not directly *to* your destination. Society today is very time oriented. People need to be at work on time. Be it socially or work related, people get together at specific times. So ironically, going without time, destination or expectation is a luxury to be experienced when it can be scheduled in, for most people.

Another by-product of always going *to* is the accumulation of more stress and worry. There's enough of that going around today as it is. Stress and worry are negative emotions that deplete our energy and distract us from being able to live each moment as it comes. As stress and worry increase, people find themselves one step from escalating emotionally to anxiety, frustration and anger. In that state of emotion, people are more prone to act erratically. When you drive with the mind-set of moving *toward* your destination, you notice ahead of time when someone is constantly shifting lanes as they come up behind you or are driving fast in the slow lane on the highway.

When you can travel without hurry, you see more of the landscape around you and maintain an alert, calm attitude. That might seem hard to do, but the benefits are worth the effort.

When you do get a chunk of time and want to take the opportunity to travel without time, destination or expectation, wandering the landscape can be an incredible teacher and a powerful way to connect with nature. The caretakers at the Tracker School, who live and practice primitive skills in the Primitive Camp for one year, have certain duties and goals to accomplish during their stay. One element in their job description is to wander the Pine Barrens for extended periods of time.

By wandering without time, destination or expectation, with the focus of moving *toward* the direction you choose, you are open to investigating whatever catches your attention and allowing yourself to be sidetracked. When you add wide-angle vision to the walk, your awareness expands even more, and you pick up on the most subtle movements that happen around you. After walking for a few minutes in wide-angle vision, you feel a shift in your awareness, your step is slower and your sense of connection with the environment grows stronger.

Often what draws your attention—a flowering bush, a large tree, a group of rocks, an animal trail or a set of tracks—becomes a teacher. Allow yourself to take side trips and go up to the things along the way that draw your attention. Ask yourself why this particular thing or place has drawn your attention. Stopping and sitting somewhere for a while, taking in the natural ebb and flow of sounds and motion, allows you to go deeper into the moment.

Because we are always receiving communications from the world of the Force, the Spirit That Moves In and Through All Things, these communications often come from natural entities around us. Plants, trees, animals, birds, a change in the breeze, you name it—these communications can come from anywhere and anything. By opening yourself to everything around you, allowing yourself to be drawn to things that interest you or catch your attention, you open yourself to the moment. Suddenly, you are not fast-walking up a mountain, but walking slowly in what I call one-quarter time, each step taking four times as long as your normal step as you immerse yourself deeper in the moment.

Wandering through a natural area for even a few hours is a great way to connect with nature. Changing your perspective and the way you move—from walking along to crawling through brush and following an animal trail, to lying on the ground and studying a track or watching insects—opens up your senses and perceptions to the world you are moving through.

INNER FIRES OF EXISTENCE

When Grandfather talked about the inner fires of life, he often referred to them as the inner sparks of existence in all things because he believed there is no separation between living and nonliving. Everything has this internal spark of existence and is thus connected with every other entity through the Spirit That Moves In and Through All Things. Grandfather explained that there is an overall consciousness of fire, or energy, in all things. That everything has an energy field was proven scientifically with Kirlian photography, in which the energy fields of humans and plants are captured through a photographic process.

One way Grandfather used to illustrate the inner fire of life was with the sandpiper. Really any flock of birds would do, but Grandfather was drawn to the small beach bird with its incredible versatility of movement.

Grandfather, Rick and I had walked to an estuary close to the bay where he had an outpost camp. We were deep in the reeds, among many different kinds of birds. The tide was out, revealing mud flats where thousands of sandpipers were feeding all around us. Occasionally they would rise into the air, swirl around, mill together, then return to feeding.

As we moved back toward our camp, Grandfather pointed back

to the bay. We watched the sandpipers rise again in a continuous wave of motion, forming into a mass of birds, all moving in synchronicity toward the ocean. In an instant they changed direction, and all their breasts flashed toward the sun as they flew south. No one bird seemed to make the decision; they all moved together. Grandfather said to Rick and me that the same spirit that moves between the thousands of sandpipers flows through everything else in creation. That is the way we are all connected, through the Spirit That Moves In and Through All Things, or the Force, as Grandfather also would use the Taoist word for the life force.

To watch a flock of sandpipers fly together at the beach is to witness a small miracle in how all the birds at once, without a signal or leader, change direction together. They can turn at sharp angles due to their small stature and spearpointlike wings, and they make their turn in total harmony. It's like watching a cloud of birds flowing together, the overall shape morphing into new shapes as they progress. Then the whole flock is suddenly flying in a totally different direction. How but through an inner connection between each one of them could this happen? This phenomenon has been observed through slow-motion photography. No one bird can be identified as leading the change in direction; there is a common instinct or sense that connects the flock together.

Grandfather said when something goes extinct, their loss diminishes the fire that burns in all of us. Though we might not know how or why, or see the direct implications of it at first, an extinction event takes away one element of the inner fire of all things. The whole of all things cannot be healthy when a part of it is hurt.

When Grandfather talked about that inner fire, he also talked about the passion of living, the spark that inspired the master craftsman to express himself through his work, the inspiration that the artist draws from during the process of creation, the love between family members and close friends. They all are an expression of that inner fire.

Grandfather talked about the Spirit That Moves In and Through All Things as being the fires of existence. That was when he went on to explain how when something dies, it is consumed by us and becomes part of our fire. Like the deer you eat will always move within you, will always be a part of you. The hunter is saying to the deer, "You will always feed my people and be part of them." This is part of the prayer of honoring.

It's even more than that when you look at the collective fire that burns in everything. When anything is hurt, when anything is lost, when anything is damaged or polluted, it diminishes that overall fire. So the human condition is affected in ways we can't measure, but we can feel it inside ourselves. We're connected to the most microscopic organisms on the planet in a very profound way, and we cannot deny that connection. Science knows that each state of life depends on every other state of life. We cannot be healthy, happy and whole if everything and everyone are not healthy, happy and whole. From the sparrow that falls and dies on the ground, to the child starving in Ethiopia or Syria, a part of us dies with them, part of our fire is diminished.

We're not looking at the fire as just a physical entity. We're looking at fire as a metaphor for so much else, for a much larger connection than most people ever imagined, a grander definition of the fires of life. Right to the fires that burn in the heart of our Earth. They are all part of the bigger picture. The reason our soils today in many cases are so rich is because of the great actions from the heart of our Earth Mother in the past. The volcanic ashes spread throughout the Earth, bringing with them the nitrogen and other beneficial elements that enriched our soils of life.

This information about the fires of existence was a conversation Grandfather and I had up by the fire in my camp. I had just brought a rabbit in that I had killed on the hunt, and he asked me if I'd prayed for the rabbit giving up its life. I told him that I had, and he said, "Good. I'll pray also. Not that your prayer wasn't good enough."

That was when he brought into that prayer the great fires of life and the fact that the rabbit was going to become a part of us, a part of our food, and would run with us forever. The rabbit's life was not a wasted life, and one day we would lie down on the Earth and return our fire to the Earth—not our spiritual fire, but the fire of the flesh.

Grandfather's explanation made me see that to kill an animal and not utilize all of it was blasphemy. By killing an animal and having it become part of you forever, you kept that animal alive. He went on to say how the same was true with all plants and whatever gifts of nature we took in to nourish ourselves. They became a part of our fires of existence and lived on through us.

GRANDFATHER LEARNS CARETAKING

Every day spent with Grandfather always consisted of three different areas of focus we soon learned to expect he would have us do. There was always a lesson in spiritual practice, a hard workout for the body and teachings in awareness, tracking and primitive skills.

One particular day was eventful. I was exhausted, and at the same time, I felt a deep sense of inner peace while sitting by the fire. I was still thinking about what Grandfather had said earlier about how the spirit of an animal or plant lived on within us and became a part of us. That evening, as we sat around a small campfire after the day's activities, I was feeling humbled from the lesson earlier that day and asked Grandfather how he had learned so much about becoming a caretaker and healer of the Earth.

Grandfather paused for a long moment, a faraway look came into his eyes and he then began to relive the story of how he had learned the skills of caretaking and healing Earth Mother from his great-grandfather, Coyote Thunder. The story was a long one, and I was shocked to find that Grandfather too had struggled to understand his place in our natural world. He also had had to learn to get through his feelings of separation between himself and nature.

When Grandfather was in his midteens, there was an ancient tree the elders simply called the Grandfather in some woods near his clan's camp. Grandfather often went and sat under this tree, which felt special to him and was a place he often went to reflect or think about a problem he was trying to find an answer to. He would often talk to the tree as if it were his closest friend. So far he had never had any communication from this special tree, but this didn't matter to him. He felt in awe of the tree, and just sitting under the tree filled him with a sense of contentment, even joy. To Grandfather, this ancient being represented nature's awesome power.

Grandfather would share his failures and triumphs with the tree. He felt a growing bond with the tree and soon could sense the tree's changing moods and how they would change as the weather changed and the seasons progressed. The tree's moods would shift between day and night. Grandfather could feel the tree's fear when approaching storms brought strong winds and lightning. He felt the tree's joy in the bright sunshine and its soft blessing in the rains. Grandfather would sit with the tree for long periods of time, sometimes even sleeping beneath its massive protective branches. One night when sleeping beneath the Grandfather, he had a dream that changed forever his understanding and perception of nature and man's role in it.

His strong connection with this tree often led him to it when he felt troubled. He felt troubled that night, wrestling with a problem that had been bothering him for some time. Even though he knew how to collect things from nature in a sacred manner, in a heartfelt way, praying with appreciation and thanksgiving, he still felt conflicted when he had to take something from nature to use for a skill, food or medicine. Yes, he felt the pain of taking a life and honored and gave appreciation and prayers each time he needed to collect something from nature, but Grandfather felt that there was more, that he was missing something. He saw that, for survival, man would take from all that nature created. The wood and brush for shelters and tools, the plants for food and medicine, the animals that fed and clothed the tribe—all were taken from creation. As he struggled with his thoughts deep into the night, he laid his head back against the wide trunk of the tree, and as he let himself finally relax, he fell into a deep sleep and entered a dream that changed his life.

The dream began with disjointed images, unconnected and random. Then these images became a horrible dream, a nightmare that shook the core of his existence. Grandfather's dream began with images of past survival situations he had experienced, of the trees he had cut, the plants he had collected and the animals he had killed. As the dream began to become a nightmare, plants and animals began to scream at Grandfather's approach. He could feel the plants bending away from him as he came close to them. Any animals he encountered ran away from him in a blind panic. He felt as if he were a disease infecting nature with his every step, as if man was a mistake of creation, a dangerous entity, totally out of control.

Grandfather's dream became more vivid, and the scene shifted. It was not only the destruction that he caused; it was the wanton destruction of the white man, which was greater than he could ever imagine. He saw the forests being burned away to make fields for crops and people living in boxy structures, their trash and waste randomly scattered about. The streams near the towns were turned toxic by the people's poor hygiene, and animals were killed only for their skins, their bodies left to rot where they had fallen. The white men's attitude for the land held no reverence; they seemed only to care about what they could take from it, never considering what they might give back to the land. Grandfather could feel creation's suffering as pristine valleys were turned into barren landscapes. The land did not matter to these people; they did not follow the laws of creation in whatever they took from the land. What mattered to them was only the present; they never considered what would be left for their children and grandchildren.

Grandfather began to clearly understand the difference between how his people survived as compared to how the white race survived. He was able to let go of some of the guilt he had been feeling, knowing there was a disease on the land far worse than he. It became clear to Grandfather that the animals and the birds could escape the ravages of man, but the plants were vulnerable and helpless to escape man's destruction. It was then the dream took another turn, to that of the old tree he slept beneath.

Grandfather was looking at the Grandfather from a distance, and he could see the approach of many people. They were loud and boisterous, crashing through the brush and carrying axes with them, all moving toward his special friend. Grandfather could feel the spirit of the tree tremble in fear and helplessness, locked deep in Earth Mother by its extensive root systems, unable to escape. Grandfather knew the approaching horde was intent on destroying the old tree.

FIRE

The people began to rain blows on the tree's trunk, cutting and hacking at its wide girth. Huge gashes were cut into the trunk, and instead of sap dripping from the cuts in the trunk, blood began flowing out of its wounds. Grandfather, to no avail, screamed at the people to stop. They either couldn't hear his cries or just completely ignored his pleas, intent on felling the old tree. The tree cried out in pain, but the tree cutters could not hear its cries. The dream went on and on. Grandfather's feelings of helplessness grew, and he felt deeply ashamed of what these fellow human beings were doing. Grandfather wanted to go down and stop them, but he feared for his life, so vicious were they in their single-minded destruction. Seeing that they would not be able to cut down the tree, some began climbing the tree and hacking away its branches. There too blood dripped from the branch stumps as the tree's cries of anguish and pain grew even more intense. Still the woodcutters paid no attention to the tree's suffering, cutting and hacking at whatever they could reach.

Finally Grandfather could take it no more. The tree was his friend, his Grandfather. To stand by and watch the butchering and suffering was more than he could bear. Disregarding his safety, Grandfather began to run toward the destruction, willing to give his life if it meant saving the life of his friend. He began pulling people away from the tree, but each time he would pull one person away, another would appear. It was like an endless stream of people whose sole purpose was destruction.

No matter how many people he pulled away from attacking the tree or how loud and frenzied his pleas for them to stop, the destruction continued, and Grandfather was helpless to stop the destruction. Grandfather collapsed in exhaustion, admitting his failure as he felt the weakening cries of pain coming from the old tree. The people felt none of the tree's pain, heard none of its cries and felt neither reverence nor remorse for what they did. They seemed to feel nothing at all. The cutting went on all through the day, and as the sun began to set, the people gathered a small amount of the wood that lay around the tree and departed, leaving the dying tree and the bulk of the cut wood behind.

Grandfather crawled to the base of the tree and wrapped his arms around the trunk as far as he could reach, feeling the life force leaving the tree, its cries, the pain of its torture as it slipped away into death. Grandfather had truly lost one of his best friends. His wailing cries woke him from his nightmare as they echoed across the still dark landscape.

Grandfather turned and placed his hands on the tree's trunk as he came to realize his nightmare had all been a dream, not the reality the dream had felt at the time. Still shaken deep inside from the powerful emotions that shook him to his core, he tried to ground himself with the feel of the tree's rough bark under his hands. The tree had not been destroyed, but it was hard for him to let go of the feelings the dream had evoked. Grandfather felt a strong urge to protect the tree, to become its guardian, to keep watch over it, to keep anyone from committing the atrocities his old friend had suffered through in his dream. But then what about the rest of creation? Could he protect it all from the destruction of man? He suddenly realized his frustration went deeper. Grandfather couldn't separate himself from the wanton destruction other men inflicted upon the Earth. Was it possible the Great Mystery had made a mistake by creating mankind? The destruction inflicted on the natural world by humankind, with its never-ending hunger for Earth Mother's resources, was like a disease consuming the host body till it died, killing the disease as well. Grandfather realized his dilemma stemmed from his feeling that he too was part of the human disease infecting the Earth.

In a sense the dream was a reflection of the inner struggle he had been experiencing before he had fallen asleep. He had to take things from nature to live, just as others had to take whatever they needed. Of course the way he went about cutting a sapling or taking an animal for food, with prayer and thanksgiving, was something the white man never seemed to do. He wondered if the plants leaned away from him like they had in his dream? On some level, he felt that he was part of the problem, that all mankind was a disease to the world of nature. Grandfather began to hate himself for being a part of the human race.

Grandfather struggled with his conflicting emotions, the self-doubt he felt as to his purpose in life and the horrific emotions left over from the previous night's dream. He was deep in thought, trying to find answers to many questions, when he was startled back to the present moment by Coyote Thunder sitting down next to him. Grandfather could not believe he had not even noticed Coyote Thunder's approach, his focus had been so completely on his emotional crisis.

Coyote Thunder did not speak; instead he searched Grandfather's questioning eyes. It was as if Coyote Thunder could see into Grandfather's heart and knew just what was bothering him. Coyote Thunder began to tell him how he too had come to this tree many times in years past, struggling with the same questions Grandfather now faced. He too had a dream reflecting the vulnerability that this tree or any tree faced due to its inability to avoid the dangers that came from man, intense storms or forest fires. A tree was vulnerable to any danger due to its immobility. He went on to say that the Grandfather was like a doorway, a portal to these questions. Anyone who came to the old tree and opened himself to it was given the same questions and the same answers.

Coyote Thunder motioned for Grandfather to follow him, and they spent the better part of the morning traveling to a mountain gorge with a stream running down its center. Grandfather could tell his great-grandfather was very familiar with this particular gorge and had been here many times in the past. Grandfather knew in his heart this place was special to Coyote Thunder by the reverence with which he led him up the mountain gorge. As they walked on, Grandfather became aware of the landscape changing even more dramatically. On one side of the stream, the forest was healthy, in balance and beautiful, while the forest on the stream's other side was not in balance. There the trees were not as healthy; many of the trees were diseased, twisted and fallen, and their branches littered the landscape. There seemed to be no natural balance in the forest on the other side of the stream. The higher up the gorge they traveled, the greater the contrast between the forests on either side of the stream grew.

Grandfather tried to figure out why on one side the forest was so healthy and on the other so sick and unhealthy, especially when all that separated them was a thin stream. Try as he might, Grandfather could not figure out what could have caused such a stark contrast between the two sides of the forest. Coyote Thunder said nothing as they continued to walk higher up the bank of the stream. The farther up they walked, the worse the contrast between the two parts of the forest grew. On the opposite side, the forest appeared as if it could barely survive, while the forest on their side grew stronger and healthier with each step they took. On the stream bank they traveled, the forest was abundant with fruits and berries, and animal runs were full of tracks from the many species Grandfather could see lived there. Still Grandfather could not detect the reason for one side being so healthy and the other so sick and out of balance.

Finally, Coyote Thunder motioned for Grandfather to sit down, and they sat in silence while Coyote Thunder's gaze embraced the forest with an expression of pure satisfaction. Then he began to tell

Grandfather the story of these two sides of the forest. He told of how in his youth this was the place he would visit to collect saplings for bow staves and arrows. Now when he came here, it was only to honor the forest. Grandfather looked in amazement at the forest. Coyote Thunder had made this place one of beauty and balance. Grandfather told Coyote Thunder he couldn't remember ever having seen anything like this place, so vibrant and healthy. Coyote Thunder gave a warm smile and said this was only one of the forests he had helped.

Coyote Thunder then began to explain to Grandfather man's purpose on Earth. He said, "Man is the tool of the Creator and of creation. Man can help nature do what would otherwise take many years. Man belongs to the Earth, and the Earth belongs to man. It is not just taking from the Earth and giving nothing in return. As you see, this forest first gave to me, and I in return helped it to grow stronger. Man has an important part in creation, for it is through man that nature can grow strong and healthy. Do not the winds and storms trim the trees? Do not animals eat the plants and other animals? Do the plants not feed on the sunshine, the soils, and the waters of the Earth? We all need one another to survive. But there must be a balance and harmony with man and nature. The forest here shows such a balance; it is the perfection of man's purpose."

Gazing at the forest, Grandfather saw the results of Coyote Thunder's efforts to create a place that was thriving. A forest in balance, strong and healthy. Grandfather began to understand what Coyote Thunder meant by man's purpose and responsibility as a caretaker of the land. As if knowing what else was on Grandfather's mind, Coyote Thunder continued, saying, "White man is not a caretaker of the Earth, but more like a disease that destroys the places he infects. He does not understand the balance and harmony nature needs to thrive. By taking—with little regard for nature's balance—and not giving back, white man does not consider how his actions destroy what his future generations will need from nature. He thinks only of his immediate survival, not how his greed to consume acts as a sickness on the natural world. By disregarding the laws of nature, they leave no legacy for the future."

As he pondered Coyote Thunder's words, Grandfather thought of more questions he needed answers to. Before he could speak, Coyote Thunder continued, "All things in nature depend on the chain of life to live. They all must feed in one way or another, taking from nature what they need to live. Man must also take from nature to live, but it is the way we take these things that makes the difference between being a caretaker or a disease. The key to living life as a caretaker is taking only what is needed in a sacred manner. By taking things with an attitude of great thanksgiving and appreciation in our hearts, we benefit the land instead of destroying it. We always see into the future and ask ourselves how our actions will benefit future generations, thinking beyond the present moment and action. Thus we will fulfill our destiny as caretakers of the Earth by leaving creation better than we found it to begin with."

After a short pause, Coyote Thunder said, "Taking things from nature in the right way is only one part of our role of living as a caretaker of the Earth. We must also become protectors of the Earth. We must be willing to defend it with our lives if needed. Nature needs our help all the time, not only when we need to take things from it for our survival. This means we must always be conscious of our role as a caretaker for we can perform many tasks to help nature that nature cannot do for itself. As we move through the world of nature, cutting, pruning, planting, helping nature along, seeking to restore its balance when we encounter situations in nature that only we can make right, accelerating the healing process or cutting away diseased parts and opening areas that are choked and overgrown. People are also part of the natural order, so we must help them grow stronger, teaching them the sacred ways. This is the best way we can protect that precious gift of life for future generations. The fight can become long and hard indeed, as many people will not listen, knowing no other way."

As Grandfather digested all that he had just heard, Coyote Thunder sat in silence, allowing Grandfather the time to piece everything together in his mind and heart. After a long pause, Coyote Thunder spoke again. "We are a people of simplicity, not excess and convenience. We only take things we need when there is an extreme need. White man's consciousness of excess and convenience comes from a place of greed that ultimately destroys the Earth. In seeking to make his life simpler and easier, the white man seeks more convenience, easier ways to live. This is not the true way, for the more white man tries to simplify, the more complicated his world becomes. He looks to the false gods of the flesh for the things he believes will satisfy and provide comfort, but in those gods, he only finds pain, inflicting his will on the natural world. There can be no satisfaction in a world of excess and destruction, only the desire for more. Our people can justify our existence through actual simplicity and, by doing so, help nature grow stronger for now and in the future. We always are asking ourselves how our actions on the land will leave a legacy for future generations. The white man thinks only of the benefit he receives in his present moment, thinking only of themselves, never giving back."

While Grandfather was deep in thought, his mind full of all that had been revealed to him, Coyote Thunder silently stood and walked back down along the bank of the stream. Feeling a new sense of peace in his heart, Grandfather began to wander the forest, in awe of the beauty and balance Coyote Thunder had nurtured through the years. Stalking Wolf then found himself wandering in the forest on the other side of the stream to better understand the stark differences between the two areas. Here the forest had a barren feel to it. There was little undergrowth, dead branches littered the forest floor, there was little diversity of plant life and the few animal tracks he did see were only passing through, leaving no signs of feeding or bedding down. He began to wonder what he could do, as one person, to bring such a lifeless forest back into balance.

Almost unconsciously, Grandfather found himself lifting fallen branches off of the few bushes and saplings he encountered, thinking about the steps he might take in this uncared-for section of the woods. He felt overwhelmed by the enormity of the actions needed to revive the area. Coyote Thunder had spent decades of his life nourishing the land across the stream. Grandfather wondered how he had begun such a monumental task. He realized one of the first tasks would be to bring in the voles, the foundation of a healthy animal ecosystem. Voles would need not only cover, but food. Certainly he could harvest seeds from across the stream and plant them in pockets of the forest. Grandfather thought of the abundance of fallen limbs and saw them as the building blocks for piles of brush that would create the cover the voles would need to escape predators. There were stands of pines being crowded out by other species, and Grandfather imagined creating a burn that would kill the invasive trees and open the undergrowth for the pines to flourish. The heat of the fires would open the pinecones, releasing their seeds and strengthening their community. The ashes and charcoal from a burn would also fertilize the soils, making them richer for new plants to flourish.

As these steps ran through his mind, he realized the task of bringing back balance to the area was not such an overwhelming one; it was simply one that would take a period of time and effort, focusing on one step at a time. A feeling of hope and satisfaction bloomed in

Grandfather's heart with the realization that he too was beginning to live with the heart and mind of a caretaker and healer.

With these thoughts fresh in his mind, Grandfather felt a pull to return to the Grandfather again, so he turned and began to walk down the path beside the stream. As Grandfather came in sight of the Grandfather, he could see a seated figure leaning against its massive trunk. Coming closer, he was surprised to see it was Coyote Thunder who sat there. This could only mean that there was more Coyote Thunder had to share about the inner struggle Grandfather had been wrestling with.

As Grandfather sat down against the Grandfather, Coyote Thunder began to speak. "Grandson, for many years you have learned the way of the spirit and the way of nature. Your quest for the knowledge and the wisdom of these worlds has been deep and passionate, and many truths have been revealed to you. What you have failed to do is see the world of spirit and the world of nature as one entity. No longer can you separate the two, for when you view them as separate, you cannot live and experience the world around you in a state of oneness. Only when you bring together the way of the spirit and the way of nature can there be no separation of self. Nature becomes a doorway to the spirit, and the spirit becomes a doorway to nature."

The sun was sinking slowly behind distant hills, and the last rays of sunlight lit the highest part of the Grandfather's canopy, turning the branches and foliage a reddish-golden color. Coyote Thunder stood and opened his arms, as if embracing all the land around him and spoke a last time. "To be a caretaker of the natural world and a healer to the places where man's destruction has created imbalances in nature is how the children of the Earth give back for what Earth Mother and creation have given to them. Through selfless actions, doing for nature what it cannot do for herself, we can accomplish, in our brief lifetimes, what the natural world would take generations to complete. The rains, winds and time will eventually trim a dead branch from a tree, while we can make a clean cut, close to the tree's body, making the tree healthier and more productive.

"Wherever caretakers and healers travel, they are always asking themselves, 'What happened here? What can I do to make this situation stronger and healthier?' When taking something from nature in a sacred way, nothing is lost. The spirit of what was taken becomes a part of your flesh and spirit. No real death occurs. Only when things are taken with no regard for the life force, taken through greed and selfishness, do the spirits of all destroyed in that taking die. The more you can bring together the worlds of spirit and the natural world, embracing the sacred oneness, the deeper understanding and knowing you gain about what acts of caretaking and healing are needed in particular areas. That is when you will be a living extension of the Creator and creation. The more you act from a purpose beyond self, your actions become an extension of your vision, as a child of the Earth, a caretaker and healer."

Coyote Thunder then placed his hands on the Grandfather, fingers spread, and stood for a moment in silent prayer; then he turned and began his journey back toward their camp. Grandfather sat for a long time, digesting all the lessons of the day, a new sense of inner peace and renewed purpose in his heart. The moon was high in the sky when Grandfather too made his journey back toward camp, stepping upon the Earth with a lighter step, taking in the night sounds around him as he journeyed home.

Grandfather, Rick and I sat without words once the story ended. The fire had burned down to coals, our only light except for the stars overhead. Each one of us was lost in his own thoughts. I wondered if I would be able to live my life with as much love and care for our Earth

Mother as Coyote Thunder had lived his. Grandfather certainly had taken his great-grandfather's teachings to heart. He lived the life of a caretaker and healer of the Earth.

I can picture Grandfather now, seemingly gliding through camp, his cupped hands holding a sprouting acorn nestled in a bed of mulch, his lips moving in prayer. Grandfather was letting himself be drawn to the perfect place to plant this acorn—a place it would blend into the landscape and provide food, medicine and shelter for generations to come.

5

FOOD

The elements of the Sacred Order of Survival—shelter, water, fire and food—do not exist independently. Everything is a mesh; nothing stands alone. Whether cooking food or smoking fish on a rack, both methods need fire to cook or preserve the desired food. You might be cooking a stew, the most efficient type of meal when living with the Earth. Stews are a great survival meal because all the nutrients of the plants, grains and meat that are released during cooking are held in the water stock of the stew.

When you cook a stew, you combine fire, water and food to get your end result. If the weather is rainy or windy, you'll also probably want some kind of shelter or cookshack. In that case, all four elements of the Sacred Order of Survival are combined. Food, in one form or another, is vital to all living, growing entities: humans, animals, aquatic species and plant life. The caretaker's role where food is concerned is to create spaces where food can be grown for humans and animals. I like the image of the victory gardens of World War II. With so much food being sent to our troops overseas, individuals created gardens to grow their own food during the war years. The explosion of community gardens around the United States during the past decade is positive proof that individual plots for growing food are important to food sustainability. Why not create a backyard garden whenever possible and grow foods you like and plants for the animals, insects and birds as well?

Food is closely related to the natural cycle of nature. With humans or animals, food that is harvested and preserved during the summer and fall is stored for the upcoming winter months. Some animals, like bears or groundhogs, even store the food in their body, gaining as much body fat as they can during the spring, summer and fall so they can ride out the winter months in hibernation.

Imagine a pie chart for the Sacred Order of Survival. In a slice that contains 10 percent of the pie chart are all the primitive skills you need for shelter, fire and water. The other 90 percent of the pie is the primitive skills needed for food. These skills include growing wild edible plants, stalking, trapping and using weaponry of all sorts, from making bows and arrows to creating the many different types of projectile points. I teach thirty-seven different kinds of shelter, each unique to the others, but I teach four times as many different types of primitive traps.

With growing food, a lot of energy and attention is needed throughout the entire process. First the land must be prepared; you need fertilizer and mulch to feed the crops. You have to plan ahead and collect seeds from the previous year. The garden must be weeded and watered; the plants thinned out. The Hopi Indians will sit with their corn, talk to the crops, sing to them and pray for their growth. The Hopi form a close relationship and bond with their crops. Maybe that is why they are able to grow bumper crops of corn in the middle of a harsh, dry environment. Ninety percent of your energy and skills is applied to taking care of feeding yourself and your family. The other 10 percent is used in shelter building, water collection and purification and fire making.

In the fall, three years ago, the acorn crop around the Primitive Camp completely failed. It was so bad that a class of sixty students, needing acorns as part of an herbal mixture, was able to find only four acorns after searching for days. I knew the deer around camp were in real trouble that coming winter. They faced a huge winterkill because of the lack of acorns. I had to make a decision to feed the deer or not. When facing a massive winterkill, you ask yourself if you can feed the deer and, if so, how much you feed them. The dilemma comes when you place food out for one deer and two come to feed there. If more food is not added for two deer, neither one will survive the winter. So if you choose to feed deer or other animals in the winter, you have to know what animals are in your immediate area and which animals are passing through.

That winter I decided that feeding the deer in the Primitive Camp and around my house was necessary. I knew it wouldn't make a big dent in the overall picture, but by creating small islands where the deer would survive would be beneficial.

During a normal year, that region of the Pine Barrens easily provides enough food for the deer. But due to the constant cutting of trees and the clearing of land to make room for housing developments over the past fifty years, the deer have been squeezed into smaller and smaller pockets to live and forage in. Grandfather saw this happening during the 1950s and began to take steps to help the wildlife of the Pine Barrens deal with the issue of habitat loss, creating small islands of underbrush the animals close to the Earth survived on, along with helping oak and pine trees where they would best grow.

When people landscape or lop off a section of the woods, they take away the transition or edge areas, so the landscape goes right from the developments, lawns and roads directly to the forest, with no buffer area in between. As a result, the carrying capacity of the land undergoes dramatic changes, squeezing the deer and other animals into smaller and smaller pockets of land that can support them. When these in-between areas of plant growth are taken away, you find many fallen trees along the edges of the forest because there are no transition areas to absorb the force of the heavy storms. It is these buffer areas that are most important to all wildlife, so Grandfather was constantly planting small islands of safe haven and food sources.

Taking care of areas where development had come in and taken out the transition areas leaving little food for the animals. It was like the deer were going straight from a developed area right into a swamp and then a very monotonous forest with little of the undergrowth so important for the survival of all the animals, from tiny voles to the top-of-the-line predators. Grandfather enhanced the animal food sources while creating safe havens for them.

Grandfather took it upon himself to plant small islands of forbs, meaning foraging plants and seed plants, like amaranth, blueberries and various grasses indigenous to the area, but in larger numbers. Subsequently, these microregions he created would help stave off starvation and balance out the depleted forest areas taken away by developments. This was very cool, because it was very similar to what nature would do over time, with the islands of animal habitat.

Often when Rick and I were with Grandfather, we'd be walking in a section of the woods where there was not much cover or food, and all of a sudden we'd come into an area that was rich with food and cover for the animals. Grandfather had cultivated these areas over the years, all on his own. He would look for an area where a couple of big trees had come down, and then he'd open up an area to receive sunlight. Grandfather would cut out the dead trees and thin areas that would eventually choke themselves out. He would then put in the lower-browse plants, focusing first on the voles, who live closest to the Earth, and proceed up the food chain to the deer and larger herbivores. As mentioned, voles are indicator animals. Where there is a healthy population of voles, you know that pretty much every other type of animal is present in that area.

For the first thirty years of the Tracker School, classes were held at an old farm in western New Jersey, near the Pennsylvania border. The old farm was a mecca for animals. We made sure that what wasn't corn or soybeans was an intense wildlife habitat of everything we could find that the animals ate, from clover to amaranth. All the plants that we can eat, animals can eat, so it's like one hand washing the other.

At that time Frank and Karen Sherwood were the head instructors, and Karen, one of the top herbalists in the country, was meticulous about making sure that things were planted and harvested in the right way. On the last night of each Standard class held there, the students, under Karen's guidance, would harvest enough wild edibles to make a salad that sometimes fed over a hundred students. But it didn't begin or end there, as the area around the farm was rich in wildlife.

Around the old farm, the area was abundant with food, cover and water sources. The carrying capacity of the land for the deer was so rich, they needed only about one square mile to find everything they needed to survive year-round. This is a stark contrast to the area around the Primitive Camp near Waretown, New Jersey, where the deer need about ten square miles of forage and cover to survive. The deer having to travel so much farther to find food and cover near the Primitive Camp, which all relates to the carrying capacity of the land. You can't take land with a low carrying capacity and turn it into a Garden of Eden, but you can take certain regions and turn them into a Garden of Eden.

In order to know what animals live around the area you live in, you need to learn what signs different animals leave, where they are traveling to and from, what they eat and where the transition areas are. If your area is poor in transition areas, the challenge is to create these areas for the animals that would normally inhabit that area. In order to learn these things, the first step is to take a sort of census of the area. To do this, sign tracking will tell you all you need to know.

SIGN TRACKING

When Grandfather taught us what a transition area was made up of and how to discover what animals inhabited or traveled through it, he told us that sign tracking was all we needed. He also said sign tracking is the easiest of all tracking. Sign tracking is everything that indicates an animal's presence other than its tracks and the footprints themselves. These indicators include trails, runs, push downs, beds, dens, rubs, scrapes, scat, animal hairs, gnawed vegetation, flagging of leaves, broken twigs and upturned stones. Grandfather told us that once we had observed the signs left from an animal's presence, then we could use their tracks to confirm what we already knew from the signs.

So how do you sign track, and where do you start? It's always good to look at the big picture, the overall area, to begin with. One way to do this is to imagine you are an eagle, flying high above the land, tracking the landscape itself, searching for the islands of growth. Imagine a map of the ground from the air. Flying in from above, you see the meadow, you see the valley and you see the differentiation of the hills. With those hills comes erosion. With the erosion comes a disturbance. With disturbance comes edge. Edge or transition areas are the places between meadows and forests, between waterways and fields. These islands are a concentrated area with a wide variety of vegetation. Transition areas also have good cover, meaning shelter for the smaller herbivores. Water sources are another thing to consider when determining how good a transition area is. When you find a rich transition area, then you're ready to explore and assess its animal life.

A lot of the time with herbivores, you don't need to think about water because they get their water from the vegetation that they eat, especially in the early morning when dew covers the vegetation. That's like the sacred order for animals. A wide variety of vegetation provides good cover for shelter and water. It's the caretaker's responsibility to learn what the animals in the area are eating, what they prefer to eat and what they can't get. By knowing what foods they prefer, the caretaker can then propagate more of those plants and expand the food sources. Consider the thousands of seeds one plant can have. You don't take them all; one spike of the plant will provide enough. Then you physically plant them and space them out, so suddenly next season, you've got a piece of real estate that has ten times the volume of that plant species.

Animals congregate around these islands because the food and cover are there. It starts with the herbivores. Since a healthy vole population is a key indicator of a good transition area, begin in the grasses and gently poke around, looking for their tunnels. The voles live between the hard ground and the litter on it. If their runs and tunnels are easily found and plentiful, you've found a good transition area. When you have a good variety of herbivores, the carnivores will follow.

A good way to get started is to select a small piece of a transition area and use sign tracking to evaluate which animals are using the area and passing through it. In transition areas, animals need cover to get out of the weather, as protection against predators and for a wide variety of food. The type and variety of available food will dictate the sustainability of the area for animals. It's also important to learn and understand the food preferences of the animals that live or pass through the area. This can be done through sign tracking as well. That is of major importance, as the animal tracks are only to reaffirm what you already know from the signs. With sign tracking you look for the big and small, the macro and micro evidence of animal behaviors.

The first step in sign tracking is to look for the animal trails and runs that move through the area. First seek out areas that include a variety of grasses, areas of heavy brush, forbs and trees. These elements together mean there are food and cover for the animals. You also want to evaluate the area for water. Don't just consider streams, rivers and ponds; look for seeps, puddles and springs as well.

Some trails are like superhighways where a number of different animals will use the same trails. In a medium-size animal run, skunks, raccoons and opossums will all show evidence of using it. You're not going to have deer go through this type of trail very often. Once in a while a deer might tiptoe through, but you won't find a lot of track evidence. In-between transition areas are another sort of highway used by a variety of animals. Here you may have both deer and coyote using the same trails. These trails are the back roads that get the animals to the supermarket and back home again.

Identifying the animal trails and runs then leads to examining them for the signs animals leave when using the trails. One of the most obvious signs animals leave is their scat. The scat left by an animal helps indicate not only what species it is, but the animal's size and diet. Animal hair is another sign commonly found on trails and the runs that branch off. Each trail and run tells its own story as it follows the contours of the land and the paths of least resistance. The goal of the caretaker is to unlock the story's secrets through observing the overall picture and the minute details left by the animals that travel the trails.

When observing the grasses and bushes in a transition area, look for places animals have browsed and the type of bite or chew markings on the leaves and branches. See how high or low particular animals can reach. The bite and chew marks are another way to identify the animal species that is feeding there.

Water sources the animals use also need to be taken into consideration when planning to revitalize an area.

You might also consider creating a managed burn in a small area to enhance future growth. The first thing you do is take an assessment of the overall area. The most important thing is to ask yourself, "What are the animals missing? What do they need?" and "What does the area need and where?"

In the section of the Pine Barrens we call the Maze, a lot of erosion was made by four-wheelers that were tearing up the landscape, and a lot of the shrubs were disappearing. What we found was that the animal activity was starting to disappear as well. The first thing to disappear was the herbivores; then we started noticing that the fox population and the raptors were missing as well. So in one of the Caretaker classes, we made "mouse nests," by putting together bundles of sticks, weaving them together similar to a Christmas wreath and lightly tying them together with cotton string or sisal. We distributed the mouse nests out there to provide the mice population cover. In amongst those mouse nests, we also planted grass seeds, the start of some future food sources for the mice.

Once the mice become reestablished, the raptors, foxes and coyotes will start moving back in, all because we put in a little bit of shelter and a little bit of food for the herbivores, which are on what you might call the lower end of the food chain. And everybody else started to stack up. When you find the herbivores, you can find the carnivores as well. There is that balance within ecosystems. So often we eradicate the rabbits or we take out all the coyotes, and we wonder why all the shrubs are growing back really, really thick. You wonder why and discover the rabbits were keeping the shrubs under control. You take out the coyotes, and the rabbits overproduce, and all those shrubs you put in the front yard are all gone.

So you've got to understand the animals really congregate around those edge or transition areas, which are the islands of integrity—potential, if you will. There's a high rate of energy flowing through those areas. Often streams, rivers and water bodies also create that disturbance, that edge.

So when you are in a survival situation, you ask yourself, "Where am I?" Whatever environment and type of ecosystem you are in—it doesn't matter where you are—look for the islands, and you will find the wildlife. What you should do is choose one spot, study it in great detail and know every animal that has the potential to live there. Even the migrants, like bald eagles, which don't necessarily live there all year, but come through on their migration. You should know all of them in that one spot. Once you understand the area you've studied, you can apply the principles of ecology that you've learned there, through the experiences you personally have, and then apply them anyplace in the whole world, and you can find something similar about all of those places.

(What's the difference between a blue jay and a scrub jay or a Steller's jay? They all very much act the same. They have all adapted to different forest types, but they still have the same personality. What is it about that? What this illustrates is that there are very common things that you can look for out there, and they will give you what you need.)

With sign tracking, once you get really good in one particular area, go and test out your skills in every possible environment you can, always looking for the signs left by any animals who pass through.

In general, there is no cover for animals in the woods. The struggle for sunlight between the canopies of the trees limits what light is left to reach the ground. It's the caretaker's job to create areas of cover in a wooded area. It's your job as a caretaker to bring in cover, plants and food. Through sign tracking, you've observed what plants the herbivores are eating. When those plants are in seed, the opportunity to act is available.

Take one plant and consider the thousands of seeds it has. Take one of the spikes, in a thankful manner, and physically plant it in an area you choose because of the light it receives and what the soil is like. Also don't leave out how you feel about the area. Does the area "feel right" to you or not? This is where surrender and tuning in to your instincts come in handy. Start by planting pockets of seeds that in the future could grow together without choking out the other species.

When you plant the seeds, space them out so the next season you'll have a piece of real estate that suddenly has a volume ten times the amount of the plant you collected the spike from. This is the perfect job for a single caretaker. Start by creating areas of cover and then put in the food sources.

Whenever you are contemplating creating areas of food and cover, be it out in nature or in your backyard, you face a challenge. There has to be a balance, because as soon as you draw animals in, you don't want them to wipe out everything. So it must be located in an area where some animals will get to and other animals won't.

Look at feeding birds. At first you have three or four local birds coming to the feeder. At the end of two months, you could have hundreds coming by. Imagine every backyard as a biome. In other words, what can your backyard support? If the answer is just birds and squirrels, fine, but don't forget to plant for the bees and insects as well. Plant some herbs and bee balm as well.

If your backyard borders a section of woods or a field, you can put a salt lick out there; you can find old antlers that are unusable and throw them out there. Just about every animal, from mice to coyotes, chews on antlers for the calcium. In the span of one winter, a four-point antler could be reduced to a four-inch chew toy.

This whole thing doesn't start in the summer or fall; it starts in the spring when everything is coming out of the ground and blooming. Then we have an open idea of what's going on and what's coming up.

HEALING THE EARTH, PUTTING IT ALL TOGETHER

Grandfather always had one pocket of his buckskin shirt filled with seeds. When he came to an area where the soil and light were just right, where a particular herb or plant would thrive, he would take out a handful of seeds from his pocket and meticulously plant them.

Grandfather would collect decaying wood mixed with bonemeal and fats for mulch, which he carried in a pack that hung over his shoulder. This way, if he wanted to plant a seed or a sprout or relocate a small sapling, he was prepared.

Grandfather believed that preparation was a major part of the journey, as a caretaker and in everything he did.

Whatever Grandfather did, whatever skill or project he was working on, he gave himself completely to the skill. Grandfather always seemed to be in a state of appreciation and thanksgiving, living for that moment alone.

He was always doing little things to help the Earth. If he saw that a tree had fallen against another tree and was in danger of falling to the ground, disturbing a place where an animal might make a lair, he would gently place the deadfall onto the ground where it would be less of a disturbance to any plants growing in the area.

Grandfather wanted not only to interact with the environment to maintain a state of homeostasis; he wanted to leave the area better than it was before.

Another way Grandfather would improve an area was by collecting seedlings from a place where they would have difficulty growing.

He'd reverently carry a sprouting acorn or other plant to the perfect location for it to thrive. There are oak trees Grandfather relocated in and around the Primitive Camp, where Tracker classes are held today, that are perfect specimens, thriving fifty years later. The Primitive Camp is also the site of Grandfather's main camp where Rick and I spent a major part of our youth. I still have a vivid memory of Grandfather, with a germinating acorn cupped in his hands, wrapped in sphagnum moss, slowly wandering the landscape in a state of deep wonder and thanksgiving, seeking the perfect spot for that particular acorn to be planted.

When Grandfather walked anywhere, it was as if he were floating above the Earth. He walked so slowly, with a step that caressed the ground. With utmost care, hardly ever looking at the ground where he stepped, Grandfather drifted along, in a fluid motion. Because his steps were so soft and slow, animals he passed would never startle or bolt as he passed them in his pure attitude of worship and reverence. Grandfather could always slip up on you without you ever sensing an approach, surprising the heck out of you whenever and wherever he chose to. It was as if he left no evidence of his passing on the landscape.

CARETAKER/
HEALING EXERCISES

———

INTRODUCTION

Throughout all the years I spent with Grandfather, he was always giving Rick and me exercises to do. Usually he gave us a series of exercises and missions that we had to master, each exercise building on the one before it. Sometimes Rick and I would work on one exercise for several weeks before Grandfather deemed us ready to take our next step. Sometimes we'd work on a particular exercise for months. We never knew what was coming next, as we were always working on so many projects around camp.

We always had to remember how Grandfather was a coyote teacher who never gave us all the information, only vague hints and some idea of how the end result should look or feel. It was through the exercises that Grandfather had us complete that we really came to understand a particular skill or teaching. One of the beauties of this kind of learning is that the learning never stops, no matter how many times you work on a skill.

In all the classes I've run over the years, the students have been introduced to many of the same exercises Rick and I learned from

Grandfather. One challenge I have as a teacher is picking which exercises to use with each particular class. I'm constantly asking myself which exercise would be best for that particular class at that moment, always keeping in mind what the teachings of the end goal of the exercises are leading toward. Another major challenge my students and I face is that I have only one week in which to present the lessons and skills, so it's important to make sure each student understands the formula or process of each exercise. This way students can take the lessons home and continue refining their skills. The learning never stops if you choose to practice the lessons.

The following exercises are exercises that Grandfather had Rick and me do over our years together and that I've had my students do. As you will see, some of the exercises related to connecting with and healing our Earth Mother can be practiced year after year with plant after plant or with combinations of plants. They can become a lifetime endeavor as well as lessons you can pass on to new generations. If you don't believe you have any kind of a green thumb, that's not the objective here, so don't worry. In these exercises consistency, acute observations and opening your awareness to what is going on around you are the most important skills to focus on. If you believe you have no green thumb, you might end up changing your belief system over time as you connect with plants in other ways, not by trying to grow them.

A major theme of this book has to do with opening oneself to the natural world and learning how to form connections with the Spirit That Moves In and Through All Things and the world of nature. Tools like wide-angle vision, surrender and asking sacred questions—such as "What does this mean?" "What is this telling me?" and "How does this make me feel?"—will open the door to the teachings that will come. There is really no one sacred question. Sure, Grandfather was constantly asking Rick and me, "What dis mean?" but that was only the first of a long list of questions that would come after.

Another important element to constantly be aware of and refine over time is learning how to interpret what your gut feeling is telling you. Take notice when your gut tightens or when you feel uneasy; that usually means you're getting a negative reaction to a question or a situation. Through surrendering, you can learn even more about what is causing you to feel that way. When your gut feeling is a release, you're getting a positive response to a question or a situation. Again, surrender reveals more information about the matter at hand. After a while, you will notice subtle differences in your gut feelings, as if there is a scale of one to ten, because some gut feelings are much stronger than others. As you learn from your failures and your belief system strengthens with your successes, you will learn to trust your gut feelings or instinctual feelings more and more. That in turn will rebound to the natural world around you, deepening your connection with it.

SEED TO SEED

According to Grandfather, you didn't really know a plant until you had observed that particular plant through each stage of its life cycle, from the opening of its first buds in spring to the bare branches of the plant in winter. Grandfather had Rick and me spend year after year getting to know all the edible, medicinal and poisonous aspects of the plants that grew throughout the Pine Barrens. Each stage in the plants' annual life cycle revealed more and more to us about their particular personalities. When we needed a particular herbal root in the middle of winter, we had to be able to positively identity the shape and size of that plant by its bare branches. We had to know how the buds of the next spring would mold themselves to the stem and their particular growth patterns, as well as how the bark felt and the subtleties of a plant's winter color in order to be absolutely sure we had the right plant.

To do this exercise is to make a long-term commitment; maybe it will turn into an ongoing one you practice for the rest of your life, as new plants come to your awareness. One year of observing a plant actually goes by too fast in some ways. Particular stages happen over a period of a few days, like when the plant is in full bloom. The leaves of a plant also go through their own stages, from when they first open in the spring until the branches are again bare, with the leaves resting on the ground below.

In your area, select a plant or several plants you feel drawn to for some reason. The beauty of this exercise is you can begin it at any time. It might be wintertime, and the bare branches of a particular plant you are not familiar with attract your attention. In any case, if you know the plant or not, choose with your gut feeling; allow your instincts to guide you.

It's a good idea to record your observations of each plant in a journal. Each type of plant has its own cycle of growth; some come to bloom much earlier than others. The weather plays a role as well by creating conditions that determine when the plant chooses to begin to bud out and come to flower. Each season of the year goes through stages in association with the weather patterns. Recording these observations is even more important in the times we live in, with more frequent variations between warm and cold fluctuations. It's important to note how these fluctuations in temperatures are affecting the plant cycles you are observing. Winter warm spells that now occur in normally cold times, quick swings in temperature and late-season hard frosts can play havoc with plant cycles. A journal that records not only stages of the plant's development but also the accompanying weather patterns that occur during the year blends to create a more complete picture. The journal also creates a reference point for future observations in the years to come.

If you choose to, throughout the year, take pictures to print and paste into your journal as well. As you become aware of new stages of development throughout the year, ask yourself the sacred questions "What does this mean?" and "What is this teaching me?" Each time you ask the questions, surrender and note what images, words or feelings come back to you. These observations are also important to record in your journal.

Later in the season, when the plant goes to seed, collect some seed-pods and pick them apart to observe how they are constructed. It's a good idea to package and label each packet of seeds you preserve. Then take some seeds and plant them in an area where the sun, shade, wind and rain are right for that particular plant.

MICRO-CARETAKING

Micro-caretaking is creating your own wild space and observing how all the creatures around you, from bugs, bees and butterflies to birds and animals, interact with the tiny wild place you have created. These micro-wild places can be made in a large flowerpot or in a small area of ground, two or three feet square. Another option is to create a micro-wild area in a natural setting. When you approach caretaking from a micro level, by starting small, the understanding and lessons you can learn about what most people refer to as weeds can then be appreciated and even re-created on a larger scale. What some people refer to as weeds are plants that grow wild and appear sometimes in places some people don't want them to be. Just because a plant is good at propagating itself and is abundant in an area doesn't mean that plant has no value. Oftentimes quite the opposite is true, and "weeds," once you get to know them, become important plants that are edible and provide medicinal remedies to both humans, animals, birds and insects.

In a small wild space near your home, you can easily observe what the wildlife in the area likes to eat. While some plants attract all sorts of wildlife, other plants are eaten by only a few species. With a micro-garden, you can easily import new plants to see what works best. Grandfather was a firm believer in building models of things before attempting to make the finished product. That way you can learn from your mistakes without using a lot of materials. When Rick and I learned how to make a birch-bark canoe, Grandfather first had us make a ten-inch model and then a three-foot model before we finally made a two-person canoe and, after that, an eighteen-foot canoe we could all ride in together. By the time we got around to making the "real thing," we had learned through our mistakes with the smaller models. Creating a micro-climate functions along the same lines. You start small so when you get to caretaking a larger area, you have a better idea of what might work in that area.

TWO PLANTS

For this exercise, you need to find two plants of the same species that are the same size. You might consider a plant species you are familiar with or, even better, a plant you don't know well and feel drawn toward and would like to form a relationship with. You can either find two plants near each other in an outdoor environment or have two potted plants at your dwelling, inside or outside.

This exercise is focused on building your belief system. It's a way to experience how intent is a major component of building up specific empathetic and healing energies. What you think, feel and believe can make a difference, even work miracles, especially when you have a purpose beyond yourself. Grandfather said that the further you can put any sense of gain from what you are intending to send healing energy to, the more effective the results will be. In a way, the relationship you build with your plant is an exercise in healing.

The exercise is also an exploration of your inner self: how it feels to bring energy into your core, where in your body you feel this experience happening and what it feels like to send this energy to someone or something else. Grandfather used this exercise and so many other ones with Rick and me in part for us to better learn how our medicine power worked.

In caring for the plants, you treat them equally in the care you provide for them. Water them the same. Use the same type of dirt and mulch when planting them. If they are in pots, place them so they get an equal amount of sunlight and shade.

The first step is to sit with the two plants and really look at them. I tell my students to look at them as Grandfather would have looked. Study everything about them and examine them in detail, but also step back to see how they fit into and with their environment. Then measure the plants and place a stick or dowel in the soil next to the plant and mark on it the height of each plant.

See the two plants from a place of wonder and deep appreciation and ask yourself how each plant makes you feel in your gut or inner core. Ask yourself from that place deep inside of you, in a nurturing, loving way, "How does this plant make me feel?"

After you have observed the two plants and explored how they feel to you, choose one of the plants to become the focus of your intentions. This plant is the one you will be sending positive energy to. Refer to that plant as Plant 1 and the other as Plant 2.

I highly recommend you keep a journal for this exercise. Keep a record of any physical changes that the plants are going through: Do they seem to be thriving or struggling? Record your observations about your experiences when you are bringing in energy, building it up and sending it. What parts of the process are difficult for you and which parts feel effortless?

At least one time each day—but two or more times are better—sit with Plant 1 and feel your connection to it. Form the intent to send it nurturing and healing energies. Grandfather always said to empower your vision before doing anything. You could liken it to praying, in the sense that you are stating what you are wanting to happen. In this case you want to empower feelings of health, vibrant energy and deep appreciation. Ask yourself what other types of energy might the plant benefit from and form that intent.

Feel your connection to Plant 1 deep inside of your core self, that place where your instincts reside. As you breathe in, direct your breath to that place deep inside of you. Also as you inhale, imagine energy from all around you entering and being built up in that place deep inside of you. Then place your hands on either side of the plant about a foot or so away from it and slowly bring your hands in toward the plant until they are a few inches away from it. When you are ready to send the plant energy, feel that energy your have gathered in your core move into your chest, down your arms, through your hands and into the plant. When you send the intended energy, make it flow gently into the plant. Pour your heart into the process. When you feel the flow has stopped, repeat the whole process of bringing in, storing and sending energy to the plant. Do this four times each time you sit with the plant. The more you do this, the more you will feel a special relationship building between you and the plant.

When you are building up and sending energy to the plant, stay in wide-angle vision. Then narrow the wide-angle vision somewhat, keeping the plant in the center of your attention. If you wear glasses, take them off when you are doing this. Even though your ability to see details in focus will suffer, entering and maintaining wide-angle vision will be made easier. Observe any changes in your environment that happen as you interact with the plant. If you are outdoors, do you notice a change in the birdsongs or alarm calls? Which way is the wind coming from? Notice when the wind increases or when it dies down. It's always a good thing to be intentionally aware of what is going on around you. How is everything going on around you interacting with one another? How are you and the area you are in interacting together?

I had my philosophy students do this exercise during a class held in Florida a number of years ago. At the end of one week, each student's Plant 1 had grown significantly taller during the week, and Plant 2 had hardly grown at all. The dramatic difference between the two plants at the week's end helped affirm for each student how bringing in energy intended to help and nurture a plant can make a huge difference, resulting in the students' personal belief systems and their individual healing abilities growing stronger.

Grandfather often said to us, "Belief is the strongest force on Earth, followed by Faith, but Faith without passion is no belief at all." Bring all of who you are into the process when you interact with your plant. Have fun; it doesn't have to be serious. A loving, playful state of mind is a great place to come from when interacting with your environment and when sending energy to specific entities.

SLOW-MOTION EXPLORATION

When you are walking in a natural area and you want to explore a bit and you feel an urge to learn something new, this exercise can open doors that you were not aware existed before. At some point during your walk, pause for a moment and determine a direction to head toward, a place you feel drawn to. Face any direction, take a deep breath, surrender as you exhale and ask: "Should I go this way?" If your gut releases, that is the direction to take. If you don't feel a release, keep turning in a circle, asking the question and surrendering until you get a clear release.

Then begin to walk in your chosen direction, but change your pace to a very slow walk or a slow fox walk, if you know what that is, all the while using wide-angle vision.

When Rick and I would rush to Grandfather's camp after school, about a quarter mile away, we would stop, pause and begin to walk in a slow fox walk we called walking in quarter time. The slow pace and wide-angle vision would "reset" our bodies and minds, so we were more in tune to what Grandfather called Earth Time.

Walking in quarter time seems to take you into a new dimension of awareness. You become more aware of the sounds and smells around you. Watch the play of light and shadow change as you move through the landscape. Feel the breezes flow around you; be aware of any changes in direction of the wind. Cup your hands behind your ears to magnify the sounds of the wind and bird peeps and songs; scan the environment. Then allow yourself to be open to whatever draws your attention, be it a tree, a plant, a rock or another natural object.

Once you feel drawn to an entity of nature, sit with it and observe it closely, in minute detail. Use all of your senses to observe it. Grandfather would say to feel with your vision, feel with your hearing, feel with all your senses. Gently touch the entity you were drawn to and ask yourself, "How does this make me feel?" or "What is this teaching me?" and then surrender.

Don't be surprised if you receive answers in unusual ways. An emotion or a feeling may come to you, but the answer could also come in the form of a symbol or a short daydreamlike vision. Be open to whatever form the communication comes to you in. You may not immediately understand the full message, but remember, you can make a list of words that come to you and rebound the list to find what words stand out, and the communication will be further revealed.

Before any exercise Rick and I would be sent out to do, Grandfather would always say to us, "Empower your vision." So before surrendering to whatever direction you feel drawn to is a great time to form your intent. Ask to be led to a place and an object that will clarify a question you have or that will reveal to you what you need to know. Remember, there are no limitations to what you can experience or learn.

CARETAKING STORIES FROM
TRACKER SCHOOL STUDENTS

Restoring a Clear-Cut in Norway

Caretaking has been part of my life since Tom introduced it in the Standard class back in 1992. It gave me a new purpose when I was outside in the woods and felt so very right doing it from the start. Instead of caring for one area, I did cleanups on the go, to whatever area I was drawn to. This continued when, in 2000, I moved from the Netherlands to Norway. The climate and the environment are much more wild and harsh in Norway than in the Netherlands, but nature there is not in great shape, despite the clean air and the waters. I lived in the rugged south coastal area, with steep rocky hills and small tough trees. Compared to Holland, where there is a wildlife abundance and, for example, deer are used to people and not really afraid, in Norway it required landscape and animal tracking to get a glimpse of the deer and moose population; still, sightings were rare but special. I had some special areas where I liked sitting and relaxing, enjoying the view of the landscape and the sounds of birds and water flowing by. One such spot was located in the middle of a steep slope where I could get a glimpse of the lake below and where a stream cut through a rather dense pine forest. I would see deer tracks going through and sometimes bedding in the area, but never really saw the deer. Because of the steep, rocky and rather tricky terrain, I did not feel like tracking the deer and spooking them. The risk of them breaking a leg or worse weighed more heavily than the joy of seeing them. I spent about two years visiting and sitting in that area, which in winter often was covered in chest-deep snow, making it sometimes impossible to get to where I sat in the months without snow. Some weeks I could not even get there at all because the snow had melted and frozen to solid ice.

One day in March 2004, I hiked toward this spot through the melting snow. Before I turned the corner to the side of the slope where my sit spot was located, I smelled pine and cut wood. It is a nice smell, but I always remind myself it is the blood of trees I am smelling. When I turned the corner, my heart stopped and I was in shock. The area was stripped clear of any and all trees and bushes.

I was angry and sad. The landscape was unrecognizable. Only the stream, which was struggling to flow because of all the branches that had fallen into it, gave me a sense of direction and enabled me to find my sit spot. The big pine I used to sit against was now a stump, and down below there were huge piles of tree trunks waiting to be transported.

As I sat on the stump, I felt the pain of the area. I was completely hopeless and shocked by the utter destruction around me, angry at the people who simply saw the trees as an investment and did not even bother to cut in a way that would benefit the land and make it stronger and healthier.

The trees were spaced too close to one another, and among the big pines were small oak and birch trees that were struggling to get light. Three-quarters of the trees were pines. Those trees could have grown bigger, and the landscape would have been more in harmony, with three types of trees prospering instead of one type dominating.

After raging for a while, I looked around to see if everything really had been stripped away. My eyes fell on a tiny pine, and my heart started to race. I got up and walked around. I found an oak that was two feet tall and that had been crushed by the truck used to move the logs. After I straightened it, it looked like it might survive. Going around, I found more damaged small trees that I could straighten and sometimes support with rocks to give them a chance to recover.

Over the months that followed, I visited the area weekly, cleaned the stream and supported the small survivor trees with rocks or sticks; in the dry summer months, I watered the struggling trees with water from the then tiny stream. In late autumn of that year, I planted many tulip bulbs in the areas where the soil was now covered with grasses, hoping that the next spring, people driving by on the road below would wonder what had happened to this scarred area. I hoped it would wake them up a bit and make them realize that this was a small flower protest against the way people treated their environment.

Unfortunately, the winter that followed was harsh and cold, and of the hundreds of bulbs I planted, only a few survived, and they were not really visible from the road. But on a sunny day in May, as I biked along the road below, I heard a girl shout: "I found another one!"

I stopped and climbed up the hill, and there were two families picnicking, and the girls were collecting flowers. I said hello to them and asked how it was possible to find tulips here, saying I was from Holland and would not expect that in Norwegian nature. They told me they had no clue. The men had cleared the area last year and were not aware there were tulips bulbs in this soil, so they must have survived for many years, and now as the sun reached the soil, they started to grow. I told them I felt this way of stripping the hills was a bit sad and looked ugly, but they did not seem to understand what I meant. They told me one of their fathers had planted the trees as an investment for the future, and they had harvested the timber. I told them I understood and realized there was no sense arguing my point of view. So I told the girls the flowers must be a sign that the area was happy again after the pain of losing its hair.

Over the next two years I made regular visits and pruned the small trees so they would grow stronger and wider now that the competition of other trees was gone.

Many things happened during the years after, and I put my attention to other areas.

In summer 2014, it was time to move back to Holland, and I made a final tour among all my favorite spots and areas; over the years these were many, and with only one week left, I was rushing to see them all. Many required long hikes and steep climbs, so it all took longer than I first thought. I had one day left before the move and was frustrated and sad, still a handful of places left but no time to see them all. I told a friend about my frustration and she said, "Oh, soon you can enjoy the tulip fields of Holland again so stop complaining." Then I remembered the bulbs I had planted all those years ago and decided that I would go to this hill as my last stop before leaving.

As I walked up the hill and came to the corner, I felt excitement and curiosity to see what had become of this area. When I was in full view, tears started to roll down my cheeks. The small trees had grown several feet and were lush. The stream was running, and there were many new bushes. Birds were singing, and the smell of caprifolium hung in the air. Wow, I was in awe of how nature had repaired itself. I slowly walked toward my old sit spot and the stump was still there, surrounded by blueberries. I sat down and tried to see the lake below, and then about thirty feet in front of me, a deer and her fawn got up and looked at me. I looked back at them and smiled. They slowly moved away from me, eating and enjoying the warm afternoon. Once again I realized we as humans have a purpose and responsibility to this planet to make it stronger and healthier.

Rien de Rooij

One Plant—One Flap of a Butterfly's Wing

Not living on a farm, near the woods, or anywhere near a piece of land that is not considered someone else's private property, I have access to just a few parks and my own yard. With that being said, I still have a true desire to help heal the Earth.

When on a walk, or a wander through the park, or even when taking a look over my own yard, if I spot a little plant in distress—whether medicinal, edible or unknown to me at the time—I do not look at it as a plant to pluck from the Earth to give its neighbors more room to grow. I look at it as in need of help, and I dig it up and bring it home, planting it in its own little pot so that I can nurse it back to health. I do the same with the plants I have indoors. If they are sick, or look as if they're on their deathbeds, they do not go to their graves. I uproot them only to replant to help reestablish their health.

Sometimes I have no idea what the plant is until it begins to regrow. Sometimes I know that it is a struggling dandelion or a weak plantain, but regardless of what the plant is, seeing that first tiny little sprig of green pop out of the soil or come off of the bare stem is always my happiest moment because I know my plucking, transplanting and nursing efforts have paid off, at least thus far.

How do my efforts, most of which are never seen by anyone other than my husband and myself, have an effect on the healing of the Earth? I look at each little plant that I save as the flap of a butterfly's wing, or one concentric ring. If each flap of that butterfly's wing has an effect on that hurricane, then one plant saved will of course have an effect on the Earth!

Saving plants one by one may not seem like much, but every single good deed, act of love, loving thought, *plant saved*—all contribute to raising the consciousness of the world and help to inspire other people to heal our Mother Earth.

Kimberly Klein

Caretaking in the City

Take two fish-and-wildlife biologists, accustomed to living in the wilderness or at sea for much of the year, and then give them jobs in the city and a new baby. What could go wrong? This was the situation for my husband, Troy, and me in 2008 when we relocated to Seattle, Washington, from the rural Oregon coast. Troy had been working at sea as a marine ecologist, and I worked seasonally in Antarctica, Alaska and on the Oregon coast. A great opportunity became available in Seattle, and though neither of us was much of a city person, it seemed like the best move for our careers. Knowing our weekends could still be filled with fishing in the Puget Sound or hiking and wild-mushroom foraging in the mountains, we took the chance.

We found a small brick house on a good-size lot (for the city) dominated by lawn and concrete. In the first few months we learned that it was easy to get out to the mountains in the early morning, but that getting back home in the evenings involved hours of sitting in traffic. The culture shock of city life set in. What had we signed up for?

Then came the chickens. I was thirty-nine weeks pregnant, and our nesting instincts were in overdrive. We went to the feed store *just to look* and walked out with three Ameraucana chicks. They were the gateway animal to our urban-farming obsession and the salve to our nature-starved souls. Having spent every spring and summer of our adult lives in remote field camps, we had zero collective gardening experience. However, in the six years we lived in Seattle we transformed that little tenth-of-an-acre patch of land into a thriving, productive sanctuary. We made a lot of mistakes along the way, losing plants to frost and poor placement, but we learned. We created our own ecosystem to make up for the wilderness that had become less accessible. The front lawn became an orchard surrounded by berry bushes and populated with Indian runner ducks and mason bees. The backyard was home to ten chickens, thirty-five quail, and a couple of heritage-breed turkeys. The compost generated by our flock along with a strategic crop rotation and a holistic-pest-management strategy powered a food forest of annual and perennial bounty. We supplemented the harvest from our yard with the salmon, crabs and shrimp we were able to catch in the sound on our little boat. That rehabbed lawn connected us with the land in a way we had never experienced. It taught me that nature can be found anywhere you can sink your toes into brown dirt or look up at the blue through your windshield.

We had adapted to the city and found peace in our little patch of land when we made a sudden and definitive decision to move to California to be closer to family. Our house sold quickly, and I cried more than a few tears for the birds, fruit trees and wonderful neighbors we would leave behind. After months of impatiently waiting, we found what I hope will be the last piece of land we ever call home. Our new house is a comfortable fixer-upper, but it was the land we fell for: a sunny patch of oak woodland bordering a stream and the redwoods; an edge habitat on a ridgeline frequented by mountain lions, with forest on one side and chaparral on the other. It is everything our Seattle home wasn't, but this little piece of land needs a different kind of healing. Decades of fire suppression have let fast-growing firs grow tall, shading and killing legacy oaks. Invasive vinca and ice plant outcompete the native groundcover. It has been almost two years since we moved in. Our house repairs remain on the to-do list, but the "doghair" firs have been cleared and the once dead-looking oak branches have shoots of green leaves spreading in the sun. We have the great privilege of knowing this one little piece of land so intimately that the quail don't flinch when our now seven- and four-year-old sons walk past them in the yard. Our boys know where to find the fence lizards on sunny days and slender salamanders on rainy ones. They know not to leave flip-flops on the porch or the gray fox will steal them and leave them halfway down the driveway. They know what poison oak looks like in winter when the leaves are gone but the sticks can still give an itchy rash, and they know to watch for the nettle and miner's lettuce that will become part of our February dinners. We are humbled and grateful.

Two remarkably different patches of land, both in need of their own kind of healing. Despite the differences, these two yards offered the same opportunity for our family to connect to something larger, something nourishing well beyond just the food they might yield. I think there is space for us all to heal the land, whether we tend a small plot in a community garden, pull invasive ivy along the trail in our favorite city park or spend our careers trying to protect wild places. This past weekend we planted our first fruit trees in our new yard and ordered a dozen fertile chicken eggs for the incubator. I hope we can use what we've learned to find a balance between wild and tended land, to create a place that will sustain the bodies and spirits of our family and the plants and animals that share our extraordinary little patch of Earth.

Lisa Sheffield Guy

Caretaking Through Touch

My name is Penny. I am a tracker student of Tom Brown. When I sent my article and concerns regarding the American sycamore trees I encountered in Todos Santos Plaza in Concord, California, I didn't expect my story to be published in this book, mostly because I haven't been able to heal these trees. All I've been able to do is pray for healing and share what has been happening to these trees for years.

Because of neglect and wrong thinking, metal bands and pipes to hold electrical wire for lights were mounted in the trees along the pathways of the park. In 1993 and 1994, the latest park renovations took place, so it appears the lights and wires were put up at that time. The trees have been affected by these man-made products for the past twenty-two years.

Over the years the trees have grown around and absorbed these foreign materials inside of them. Nobody cares about these trees. A few years ago I made many phone calls, but nobody cared enough to even talk about what could be done that would help the trees. There are over twenty trees like this and it's just plain wrong, but nobody cares.

I haven't been able to heal these beautiful trees except through my touch. What I mean by that is when I touch them, I get the feeling that they know I care. They know somebody is aware of what they have had to deal with.

One of Grandfather's lessons that Tom taught in a class I took was: To touch is to know; to touch is to heal. The only healing I have been able to give the trees is through my touch, my caring. They know I am their friend, and maybe, just maybe, they feel better knowing that their relatives, at least some of them, don't have to live with metal bones inside of them. My hope is that when enough people realize how the lights are hurting the trees, the right person, with the right power, will care enough to change the lighting in the park and remove the piping, metal bands and lights in a way that's safest for the trees.

I believe the American sycamore is a very important tree for a few reasons. One of those reasons is that I call them Native American trees because the American sycamore is native to North America. Another reason they are important is that in times of drought, you can tap the tree for water because the root system goes so deep. It's a good tree to get to know.

Penny Young

Return to Beauty: Stone Circle Farm

It is Sunday, February 26, 2017, in the early afternoon. I am sitting by the woodstove rereading *The Quest* so that I can better understand why I am being asked and how to respond to a person who wants me to help her do a ten-day vision quest on our land. The chapter "Fusion with Spirit" really caught my attention—so much so that I was beginning to feel the oneness. Then my wife, who was at the computer, said, "There's an e-mail message from Tom Brown." My reverie was broken. Tom talked about the new book, *Guide to Healing the Earth*, and asked if anyone had a story to contribute. An inner voice said, "Tell your story."

More than thirty years ago, we bought fifteen acres of property in southwest Michigan that were a hayfield. The owners were friends that had acquired significant acreage and were getting into the home-steading experience. They had the idea that three couples could share the work and the equipment that would help us all to live close to the Earth organically. The owners and the other couple eventually chose different directions and we (my wife and I) had to decide "Do we really want to stay on this land?"

So we walked to the center of the property and sat on the hill to decide. The words came that this was the place for us. During that decision process, I wondered about my love for trees and the wilderness. A distinct message said, "Norm, if you want a forest, you will have to make it happen." OK, we agreed to purchase the property and establish our homestead where we would grow as much of our own food as we could while leaving a minimal carbon footprint. I collected tree seeds (and still do) that would grow in the area, got them to germinate and planted them out on the land, thus making the beginnings of wildlife habitat on seven acres. Another three acres were designated to become a prairie. The prairie is maintained by springtime mowing and seems to be doing well, while we add a few different wildflowers every year. I have planted a hundred-plus trees since we took up residence and some of the trees are showing themselves above the grass. Also during this time, I was taking a bunch of classes at the Tracker School, participated in a number of Jon Young's Art of Mentoring workshops, as well as his Kamana nature connection program, and became a Vision Quest Protector under Malcolm Ringwalt's tutelage.

With retirement from the world of employment, we looked at the land again and began a shift when we realized the importance of having edible and medicinal plants growing in this botanical sanctuary. My wife has taken courses from recognized herbal masters and is learning how best to use the gifts that are around us. We continue to grow together (married fifty-two years), honor the Spirits of this place and make efforts to show others that a sustainable lifestyle can work.

Building community is a challenging endeavor, but we keep at it. Along the way, we have found a deeper understanding that we are not separate from nature and our land, but we are all part of one interdependent living organism that is our planet. We are learning to balance the outer world and the inner world, connecting our soul with the spirit that lives in all things. And we give thanks to the spirits for giving us the opportunity to share our knowledge with others.

Norm Bober

Ask the Plant

Here is a story I personally share about plants and Inner Vision:

I was in New Zealand some years ago and came upon the New Zealand "Christmas tree." It is not really this, but a tree with red blossoms and a beautiful tree. I wondered what it was used for by the Maoris. I recalled that Tom had said, "Ask the plant," and so in some inner thought process, I asked my question and opened my mind. What popped into my head was using the bark for sore throats. Tom also says to check it out, and it happened that there was a bookstore not far away with a compendium of Maori medicinal plant uses. I looked up uses and . . . yes, sore throat. I was a little off and looked further, and for this, the flowers of *Metrosideros excelsa* are used for sore throats and the bark for intestinal problems. The learning is that it can be done, that you check it out before assuming something and that maybe you are a little off but very near to true Inner Vision!

Bob Gannon

Sagebrush Steppe

More than three hundred fifty species are dependent in this large but seriously degraded western habitat. Threats include years of heavy livestock grazing, oil and gas development, invasive species and increasingly severe wildfires, not to mention hundreds of miles of abandoned fence that blocks free movement of wildlife. Volunteers are planting willow in livestock-degraded streambeds and pulling old fence. Thirteen years ago I bought four hundred acres on the cheap as it was so heavily degraded that it would no longer support viable grazing. Over the years the native grasses are returning. Frogs and toads can be heard in the high desert. Rabbit brush—not a favorite of ranchers but vital for late-season blooms for bees—is proliferating. Five different varieties of bees call this acreage home. Last year for the first time, small native sunflowers came up in profusion. The dried seed heads sticking above winter snow feed the wintering flocks of chickadees. Love, rest and natural forces aided by the judicious prayers and efforts of man can and do make a difference.

Jim Carlson

Healing the Earth

To help the Earth to heal can be accomplished in as many ways as there are different personalities. For me, I have learned through experience (and training with a Native elder) that healing best begins with healing myself and my relationships. There are a basic respect and connection with the Earth and its inhabitants that are accomplished through healing ourselves. My experiences taught me that we are all connected in the web of life through an energy that can best be described as feelings. We have the ability to communicate with one another through this energy. To truly help heal the Earth and one another, I believe, is to heal these connections.

I had a whole herd of deer crossing through my lot, regularly, in a mountainous area of Colorado in order to get to a nearby lake. After I began earning their trust, they would come and stand by my door, waiting for me to come outside. I began to recognize individual faces and unique markings and even began naming some of them. It was one of these deer that Kaylee, my granddaughter, hand-fed slices of apples to.

When I had earned the deer's trust enough to hand-feed some of them (I had lived there for five years), one day I opened my door to find a young deer standing there with a friend (deer) I didn't recognize. This friend had a huge abnormal growth above her left eye, making it difficult to see out of that eye. I immediately sensed the deer was asking me to help her friend. Although I knew I was gaining a reputation as a natural healer among the local people and their pets, I was not aware my reputation had spread among the wild animals!

I pondered the situation a bit, especially about how to apply anything so close to the eye on a deer whose trust I hadn't earned yet. I couldn't apply the ointment I had developed since I didn't want to take the chance of any oil getting in her eye. I would have to use a simple yarrow solution that I have learned is safe enough to use all the time for dry eyes, but strong enough to treat cataracts, glaucoma and pink eye safely. Most important, I needed to establish trust with this new deer first.

I didn't push any healing that day, but encouraged the deer to start trusting me by offering her a piece of apple. Her friend seemed to encourage her by nudging her to take it. The next day, both showed up, and I added carrots to their treats. By the third day I figured out a treatment to try. As I was feeding her bits of carrots and apples, I lowered my feeding hand (to get her to lower her head) and used my other hand to pour a small amount of a yarrow solution on her growth. It startled her the first time, but I repeated this method for several days until I saw evidence of the growth shrinking. One day the deer with the growth didn't show up, but her friend did, and she brought with her a new friend, who had a wound on her leg!

I make new friends with the local wildlife every day. I even carry on conversations with them. I am reminded that people can understand this relationship with a pet, and I wonder, "Why not a wild animal?" Why would they be any different? In many ways they are smarter, since they have the ability to take care of themselves, but they seem to appreciate that someone else cares about how they feel and are capable of expressing that appreciation.

For example, my moose friends who escorted me out of the forest one day, when I got caught in a lightning-and-thunder storm. I had found temporary shelter under a large pine tree. It seems the moose (male and female) found shelter under some trees about fifty yards away from me. As I'm peering through the downpour, wondering what it is I'm seeing, it suddenly dawns on me what they were. I hadn't encountered moose in these forests before, and I have been walking this area for many years (about thirty). I wondered how to let my presence be known without spooking them and possibly causing them to turn on me. The answer came to me to stand up in alignment with the tree trunk. They might think I'm part of the tree and therefore not threatening. This worked, and when the downpour stopped, I ventured beyond the tree trunk. For added protection, I used body language to express my intention of walking past them, not toward them or threatening in any way. I looked down at my feet, then toward the direction I was heading, then at them, to determine if they understood my intention. They seemed to, since they continued feeding, but I noticed the male's hair was raised slightly, as if he was on guard.

The moose walked parallel to me for a while in the forest, so I was able to get pictures. I didn't ever feel threatened. I even caught a picture of the male peeking from behind a tree and smiling at me. Just when I thought the two had gone their own way and as I stepped into the clearing of a dirt road that led into town, the male moose also stepped out in front of me. He faced me and looked at me curiously, with his head slightly tilted as if to say "I've escorted you this far. Are you sure you will be OK?" I nodded in assurance; then he nodded back, and we parted ways.

These stories were meant to illustrate my concept of what it might take to help heal the Earth and its many diverse life-forms: a connection, understanding, trust and mutual respect between all forms of life on this planet. I want to stress that I am not naive enough to think that we shouldn't kill another life-form. Something must die in order for each of us to live, but this can be done with a thankful and kind heart, understanding that someday we too will return our bodies to the Earth to help feed future generations. Many other species seem aware of this circle of life and the concept of balance and have been known to sacrifice themselves so that another can live.

How, then, do we help the Earth to heal? We can educate the people or pray for the people, but I believe one of the best methods is by sharing stories. I don't believe there are any easy answers to this question, but sharing individual experiences and the lessons learned is a great way to begin.

May we each walk in balance on this Earth, our mother.

Theresa (Tressea) Faye Leonhardt

Nature in an Urban Yard

Staten Island is a dense suburban environment. I live in a 945-unit town house development, which is mercifully adjacent to a hundred acres of forest. A lot of my caretaking is picking up garbage in the woods as I walk the dog. I'd rather the kids hang out in the woods; it's better for them to be in nature rather than on the street corner. So I carry bags in my pockets to pick up their bottles and cans.

Archaeologists of the future will be digging up my beer bottles from when I was their age. Best to pick them up.

The piece of the Earth I am closest to, however, is a small area right in front of my house. It's my sit area, where I start my day with thoughts and prayers. I began to think that I should make this little five-foot-by-seven-foot area beautiful.

Most of this little area was hard as rock. The cul-de-sac is slanted so that a heavy rain sends a river of water through it, washing away soil and leaving clay and stones. So the fact that it is a sort of dry stream-bed, and that it's in the shade, meant that nothing would grow there. Suggestions that I amend the soil, I knew, could fail. Digging it up could have it washing away in the rain.

But I remembered having a worm box years before. It was a bin of shredded wet newspaper and earthworms, which quickly digest a home's food waste. Knowing that worm tunnels would do all the digging and aeration without soil erosion, I now had a plan.

I sacrificed an M16 bayonet to dig (regular trowels would bend in this soil) just to put holes to plant hostas for a shade garden. Except for these holes, I left the rest of the garden untouched. I then dumped all of our food scraps right on top of the soil and covered it with leaves so the neighbors wouldn't know that I was basically throwing "garbage" in front of the house.

The worms then worked their magic. A six-inch mound of food scraps under leaves would slowly sink to the ground in a week or two. All of our home's food waste was digested by this little patch of Earth.

After a few years this spot is a jungle of hostas, violets and caladiums, which the neighbors compliment. Scrape away some leaves, and the soil below is now a beautiful loam like what's on a forest floor, and it's filled with earthworms, sow bugs and whatever else loves our food waste. Water from a heavy rain no longer runs through the spot but soaks in.

For the winter, when worms are dormant, I've just bought a new worm box for indoors. There is great power in coffee grinds, eggshells, fruit rinds and all the other things worms love. These things heal the Earth.

I no longer throw such good medicine in a garbage can.

Vincent DiTizio

Mentored into Adult Children of the Earth

My wife, Colleen, and I started a training school for preparing and launching young adults back in 1998. We were almost miraculously led to a thirty-nine-acre property with a two-story, five-bedroom home in the mountains of eastern Washington overlooking the Pend Oreille River.

One third of the property had been nearly clear-cut. The land looked butchered, with about a dozen slash piles and deep gouges from heavy equipment. The only landscaping was a small front yard with three small cherry trees.

Since this was a school for inner transitions, vision quests and rites of passage for college-aged students, we metaphored the inner with an outer transition of the property led by the students. The first step was to eliminate the slash piles, salvaging most of the timber for firewood, our primary source for heat. We brought in fill dirt to level out the gouges and make the land usable.

We used dead, downed and standing dead wood, cedar and log pole pine to build a natural rail fence, which became the envy of our rural road along the river. We were gifted llamas, which naturally refertilized the field and taught the students animal care (parenting skills).

We set up a ceremonial area, where the students learned how to have gratitude and connection with Mother Earth and celebrate positive life steps.

The back slashed area became an organic garden, an art-and-music area and an orchard. Activities helped students to further connect with nature and to caretake the land. By the seventh year and with close to a hundred students who had supported it, the property had been transformed from an environmental mess to a beautiful space to live and learn in and for students to design a life for themselves. They learned self-care, Earth care, common sense and sustainable skills; plus, families learned to do meaningful rites of passage for future generations.

Randy Russell

Making a Home for Birds

My name is Susan, and I live on thirty-five acres in Alna, Maine, with my husband, Thom. Of the thirty-five acres, twelve to thirteen are all hayfields. The rest is woods, which abut about four hundred acres of preserved land like ours along the Sheepscott River. Our property is listed "forever wild" to prevent it from being forested or developed further. When my husband first bought the property in 2002, the hayfields were being hayed by a neighborhood farmer who basically damaged the fields and did as many cuts as he could throughout the season without giving anything back in return.

After the first year, my husband would not allow him to hay the fields anymore and found another farmer who used more care and would only hay once a year during the second to third week of August. Then the rest was left to return back to the Earth. It took several years for bobolinks and meadowlarks to come back. Now each year we host anywhere from thirty to fifty nesting pairs of bobolinks and many other birds. After we had conversations with some of our neighbors, they too wait to have their fields hayed to give the ground-nesting birds a chance to get off a brood or two. Bobolinks are becoming scarcer here in Maine due to so many people allowing farmers to come and hay all summer. I feel honored to know they come all the way from South America to nest in our fields—not to mention the amount of bugs they eat each year. Another beauty of these magnificent fields is the colors they change to throughout the seasons—yellows, to purples, pinks and white—and then, to top it off, the hundreds of grasses that bloom, which are so very beautiful to see dancing in the breezes.

We also have eighteen bluebird boxes, which are filled each spring with bluebirds and tree swallows—such beautiful little birds. They become very accustomed to us sitting out at the picnic table and fly all around us catching bugs. A cute story from last summer: While sitting with my husband at the picnic table, I was being plagued by a horsefly that wanted me for lunch. I walked to the house for a drink, and of course it followed. A tree swallow was buzzing around, and I kindly asked if he would help me with this pesky horsefly. No sooner were the prayers out than I felt a light touch to the back of my head and poof! the horsefly was gone. It felt like the touch of an angel wing so very gentle as it swooped away from me as I turned my head. A thank-you was in order. Sorry, horsefly.

On the coast of Maine there is a two-mile nature conservancy beach called Seawall Beach. You have to climb Morse Mountain to get to it—about a two-mile hike in and out. It is absolutely beautiful, and what you carry in, you carry out, with no bathroom facilities, so many people choose not to visit this beach. The beach is left for nesting piping plovers and other shorebirds.

We have been going to this beach for many, many years; the only cleanup that gets done is once each April when volunteers remove all the lobster traps and pick up trash from the beach. The volunteers also mark out the sites that are likely nesting spots for the piping plovers. Otherwise, you can only walk the beach and swim; no playing ball, no kite flying, etc. Sounds wonderful, doesn't it?

Many years ago, we watched a couple of young people carrying out a load of stuff from the beach and leaving it at the head of the trail to the beach. Well, Thom and I knew it was our responsibility to help as well. Every time we visit the beach now, which we often do year-round, we collect a full trash bag, sometimes even more, from all that washes up onshore and what others leave behind. The people who cover the gate come down to the beach and pick up all the trash and items left and haul them out over Morse Mountain. At first people would look at us like we were weird or crazy. (They would never be seen doing that!) But now our kids and grandkids help out as well, and we now see other people doing the same, to keep this sacred piece of shoreline clean for everyone. Oh, and if you forget a bag and let Earth Mother know that you can't carry anything else in your hands because they are full, she will provide you with one. Many, many times this has happened to us, and before you've walked too much farther, you would find a bag washed up on the shore to use, such beautiful gifts. Thank you for taking the time to read this. There are such warm, beautiful places with so many memories.

May the eyes and the spirit of the eagle be with you.

Susan McCullough

Restoring Southeastern Pine
Savanna at Briery Creek

The summer of 2004 brought me to Briery Creek in Fluvanna County, Virginia, for the first time. The three-hundred-acre forest there had been clear-cut in 1992 and mostly replanted with loblolly pine trees in 1994 with the intention of having them clear-cut repeatedly every so many decades. The ten-year-old forest was struggling to grow back healthily. The landowner gave me the opportunity to take it on as a project as I began forestry school in 2005. Remembering the years I had spent looking for just such a place to practice caretaking and the skills I had learned in the Caretaker class in 2001, I set out to restore the forest and to learn along the way.

The early years at Briery Creek saw a lot of work with hand tools to slowly thin and prune the forest and to fix the roads to stop soil erosion and loss. Forestry school taught me about the extensive pine savannas throughout the southeastern part of the country, how they were maintained by the Native Americans with fire and how to responsibly use fire in the forest today. I also learned about how livestock could be sustainably integrated into a pine forest to promote savanna structure and vegetation with silvopasture. I began planning how to integrate these skills at Briery Creek to restore the native pine savanna there, and by 2010, I was raising goats and sheep to move out there and was conducting regular controlled burns. The integration of controlled burning and livestock with the caretaker principle of removing plants from the landscape in a way that improves the health of the forest has greatly accelerated the progress toward achieving savanna restoration. I now use a system developed through years of research, trial, error and revision.

The first step is to enter a thick area of forest and cut down the sick and dying trees that are overcrowded and suppressed beneath the main canopy. The next step is to clear a path around an acre or more at a time to be used for temporary sheep fencing and a firebreak. My flock of sheep, descended from the St. Croix breed, comes in and eats the foliage from the felled trees and the invasive species such as Japanese honeysuckle, Chinese privet, tree of heaven and multiflora rose. The hooves of the flock also help to pack down the forest litter to help control the intensity of the next step: the controlled burn.

Burning is done in the fall as the pine needles are shedding in areas that have been burned before, and in the summer months in newly thinned areas to help control the resprouting of woody plants and the invasives there. The goal is to burn every year for the first two or three years to obtain good savanna structure and to then burn on a three-to-five-year rotation thereafter. The flock is rotated so that it spends up to two weeks on a given patch before being moved and so that it returns to every patch once or twice per year. Trees I want them to eat are cut while the flock is present so they make good use of the leaves as forage. Stems and branches are then available for firewood, shelters and crafts for camps and other programs.

A power-line easement through the property was the perfect place to establish a native warm-season grass-prairie environment, so I spread seeds and practiced rotational grazing and burning there too, and I have watched as switchgrass, big bluestem and Indian grass have flourished along with a large variety of wildflowers. Recently, I also began planting native wetland trees around the pond and in the beaver meadows: Atlantic white cedar and bald cypress. I generally let our beavers engineer our wetlands for us, but reintroducing these two tree species to the wetlands will protect the water in key areas and provide unique character and habitat.

Today, I have transformed well over one hundred acres of Briery

Creek into healthy forest through the use of caretaking, rotational foraging by sheep and controlled burning. I expand our area of impact there every year and am now looking to acquire more land in the region to help heal other sites. I look forward to all the Earth teaches as the journey continues.

Chris Fields-Johnson, PhD

A Lesson from the Birds

When you watch the others we share the Earth with and learn the stories of their lives, you discover they are not so different from humankind. We help heal the Earth when we love them all.

If you are housebound, or mobility is difficult for you, or you are just too exhausted to move, know that I only had to look and listen as the birds in these stories visited or lived their lives in two side-by-side pine trees next to my apartment's second-story balcony.

Neighborhood Watch

A hawk lands in the crown of the left-hand pine tree, the branch he sits on bending down and the other branches hiding him, but only up to his chest. His predatory attitude is "Nothing to see here. Move along." The First Alert juvenile gangbangers of the neighborhood, the grackles, sound the alarm. Representatives of other birds (wrens, thrushes, sparrows, starlings, robins) fly over and land in the right-hand tree and yell at the hawk, letting him know, "We know you're there! You can't fool us!" The cacophony goes on for several minutes and is ignored by the hawk. A hummingbird zips around the corner, zooms by everyone and hovers just out of reach in front of the hawk. Then it does a dancy little loopy flight around, in front of, over, and under the hawk as if to say, "Dude, you're busted! We totally see you!" That was one disgusted hawk. He left.

A Lesson in Civil Discourse

Ms. Sparrow is sitting on a branch, looking around, chilling. Mr. Sparrow comes roaring up, lands next to her and, boy, is he mad. He's hopping mad. He's flapping his wings. He's jumping up and down. He's yelling in her face, chirping his little lungs out, just outraged. She looks at him, reaches down behind him, grabs his tail feathers in her beak, yanks him off the branch and dangles him upside down. Now he's screaming and yelling upside down and flapping for all he's worth. And then she lets go! He was an acrobat! He was rolling, pitching and yawing until he finally managed to get right side up and land on another branch. And he stayed there. Very quietly. Meanwhile, Ms. Sparrow is sitting on her branch, looking around, chilling.

Bully Dove

Two big doves live in the left-hand tree, two smaller doves in the right-hand tree. One of the big doves constantly flies over and wing-whacks and bullies the little doves, driving them off their eggs and out of their nest. It's a birdie war zone.

After one prolonged attack, bully dove retired to a branch on the other side of the tree trunk from the little doves and their nest. A couple of minutes later a dozen sparrows come chattering into the little doves' tree. They sit in a half circle above the big bully dove. Shortly after that, a female grackle flies over and lands on a branch in front of Ms. Bully. Two other female grackles fly in. They're all talking grackle talk. The sparrows have settled in and are quiet.

CARETAKING STORIES FROM TRACKER SCHOOL STUDENTS

The first grackle jumps to Ms. Bully's branch, sits down right next to her, looks at her and just rags on her, talking, talking and talking. This goes on for at least two minutes.

A starling flies in and, like the sparrows, just watches. Ms. Little Dove is sitting on her eggs in her nest, her mate sitting on another branch near her. Ms. Bully lowers her head, growls and starts waving her tail up and down, letting everyone know they're getting on her nerves and she doesn't like it. Not one bit.

Grandma Grackle continues talking, though, and all the Auntie Grackles chime in every once in a while. They make their point. Ms. Bully takes off. The grackles leave. The sparrows leave. The starling leaves. The little doves settle back in.

Ms. Bully has heard from a jury of her peers, in front of witnesses, and learned her behavior is unacceptable, even to others who are also territorially aware.

Renee Brown

Path of the Earth Steward

As I walked through the crystalline blanket of snow on this early March day in 1993, I saw the land for the first time in daylight. It was a handsome landscape, with undulating hills of various sizes and shapes, yet something seemed to be amiss, off-balance, out of sorts, on this five-acre parcel. There was scant physical evidence to support my feelings, but the feeling persisted. The only obvious evidence was the scrawny white spruce in the southwest corner. All else was submerged beneath the blanket of purity. Even with this cover, it was possible to discern many of the hidden details of this landscape. Trees were sparse except for on the north end, where a large population of drunken box elders staggered along the artificial arrow-straight drainage creek. It appeared that this was a wetland because of its relative flatness there. There was another small patch of wetland in the southwest corner, where cattails protruded through the snow. Further analysis of this land's condition awaited the disappearance of the snow.

The snow left, exposing the land, which now had a markedly different character than when the pure white blanket of snow lay serenely upon the landscape. The south hill sloped north and was devoid of much life, being a broad expanse of barren clay with a few blades of grass every couple of feet or so. The ground was cracked, and three small trees populated this hill: two American elms and a green ash. There was a small east-sloping hill that was completely blown out with erosion, and nothing was growing there. The former owner had mowed most of this parcel; before that, it had been farmland. Barbwire strands lined the northern and eastern borders, embedded in the ground, and passed through the trunks of some of the bordering trees. Two burn barrels sat at different locations on the landscape. One held the remnants of aerosol cans, gallon paint cans, fluorescent lightbulbs, batteries, scraps of metal and who knew what else. The healthiest-looking tree was a Colorado spruce with a split trunk.

I examined the creek with the drunken trees and discovered that root rot had caused the trees to pull out of the soft soil and tip in a slow-motion fall. The ground was waterlogged, and the spring weather brought widespread flooding to this region. There were trees growing horizontally two feet off the ground for fifty feet. Thick thatch lay beyond the trees. A small grove of trees held a majestic cottonwood, a hefty basswood, a hackberry tree, and a tall black willow on a small rise at the west end of the creek. This area was in good shape, but it was small relative to the rest of the five acres. There was another grove of box elders in disarray bordering the wetland close to the creek.

American elms were scattered around the yard, and some seemed to be afflicted with Dutch elm disease. The yard was a lawn with dandelions. A quick survey of the soils revealed that six different soils existed on this five-acre parcel: sand, loam, sandy loam, clay, clay with egg-size rocks and bog. The landscape was dominated by heavy clay and bog. This was the first assessment, and it highlighted the neglect and damage wrought on this five-acre parcel. The landscape as a whole was well situated and capable of supporting a vast array of life, yet it had a feel akin to a desert, sparse with plant and animal life.

A tally of the trees revealed that there were thirty-five species of trees, with a few of them on the invasive list. Exactly five trees were evergreens, and the rest were deciduous. Three of the evergreens were planted right next to the house, which means, as they grew, their branches would interfere with the roof. Some of the trees looked as if they were parched, despite ample rainfall. I decided to begin the process of restoring the landscape.

In the beginning, I used an entirely physical approach to address the problems on the landscape. I read extensively about the culture of trees and plants, using this information to develop a plan for curing the erosion problems and restoring the lost topsoil. I began to acquire the taxonomic names of the many plants, because they proved more reliable than the common names. The authors of these tree and plant books spoke of the personality of the plants as well as their needs and characteristics, which completely captured my attention. I was captivated with learning the many variables that influenced the growth of the trees and the understory. I had this feeling that something was still missing from my understanding, even though I had scrutinized and read around twenty books/field guides.

The answer came in an entirely unexpected way. I had a coworker I ate lunch with on an almost daily basis, and we discussed environmental topics most of the time. One January day, in 1995, he came by my office and said, "You might be interested in reading this book, but I want it back."

It was the first-edition hardcover of *The Tracker* written by Tom Brown, Jr. I devoured the book in one night and gave it back to my co-worker the next day. Here was the piece I was seeking, something I had been searching for for twenty-four years. I went to the bookstore the next day, saying to myself, "I hope this guy wrote some more books." I bought every title in the store written by Tom Brown, Jr., and ordered the remainder. I read all of Tom Brown's books within three months, and they revealed a world I never knew existed, yet it somehow seemed out of reach to me. I read many more books by other authors and finally went to my first Tracker School class in 1997. From that point on, the learning continuously accelerated, so much so that I had no clue where the end point might be. The piece that was missing, that which I was seeking, was the spiritual.

As I took more classes, I incorporated more of the teachings into the restoration of the land. I was drawn most strongly to the spiritual and integrated these teachings into the healing of the land. A process had started that was slowly beginning to take form, an understanding of the bigger picture of what bringing a landscape back into balance entails. Developing this understanding dominated my thoughts as I yearned to sort out what I did not understand. It pointed toward an answer as to why we are on this planet. I came to the realization that the path I had chosen to walk was that of an Earth steward. It was this that I needed to embrace to bring the land fully back to health.

I came to understand that an Earth steward is responsible for all things in the environment. An Earth steward is a guardian, a protector, a caretaker, a custodian, a curator and a healer. An Earth steward draws upon physical realms as well as spiritual realms. It is not possible to achieve a complete healing and restoration without both components. Using one or the other results in an incomplete restoration of balance, an incomplete healing and a less robust result. This path demands a high level of effort, but it ultimately is the most efficient approach. The Earth steward seeks out the levers that tip things in positive directions, and incorporates the inhabitants of the landscape in the active restoration and healing.

I learned that the spiritual realm communicates via Inner Vision and the Sacred Silence. This is paired with the physical, drawn from the world of science and physical experience. In both worlds, the most important thing is awareness. As my awareness of the five-acre parcel grew, there was a sadness that seeped into my heart when I looked at the land. This was early in the process, and physical actions had already begun. There was a long road to bringing the health back.

In Tom's Caretaking class, he pointed out that the work and actions would initially be split 40 percent physical and 60 percent spiritual; ultimately the work and actions would move to 10 percent physical and 90 percent spiritual as time progressed. It became very clear that the spiritual component was the heavy hitter in correcting the deficiencies, afflictions and injuries of the landscape. A purely physical approach would only result in disaster.

Using my scientific background and the spiritual tools taught by Tom, I came to the understanding that a full healing of the land must consider many interconnected variables. These include climate, toxins, erosion, invasives, carrying capacity, overpopulation, soil, water, sunlight, wind, nutrients, protection and the interconnections and links between all the elements. I was excited by this revelation, because now I understood what I must do to bring the landscape back to full health. I came to realize that anybody could do this. This was not isolated to a special enclave of select people. It was available to everyone.

At the start, when I was only using the physical, and was ignorant of the spiritual, I realized the land could not heal if poisons were around. I decided that I would never use synthetic chemicals on the landscape: pesticides, fertilizers or herbicides. I also included no watering in the actions, because I wanted the end result to be self-sustaining.

In the spring of 1993, I began the process of removing the physical toxins from the land. I was very concerned about that burn barrel with the scorched chemical containers. This was definitely not good. How far had any of these chemicals seeped? I donned goggles, a respirator and nitrile gloves and dug out all the ash, including the soil three feet beyond the burn line. I put all of it in heavy-duty bags and carted it off to the hazardous-waste site. Then I pulled all the barbed wire I could find out of the ground, because this is a hazard to anyone walking on the landscape. Along the way, I collected a variety of trash objects and recycled or disposed of them. This removed the initial layer—the first layer of physical, tangible pollutants—but many more would be discovered. The more difficult and insidious physical pollutants were the hidden chemical pollutants dispersed, dissolved and distributed within and throughout the soils and waters of the land. When I gained sufficient spiritual skills, I was told that the clearing of these chemicals would take time, my continual removal of trash and most of all patience.

When I looked at the scarred, denuded, cracked clay landscape of the south hill, I asked myself, "How do I bring this back?"

I had not read Tom's books yet when I asked this question, but I set out to come up with a solution based on research. I was quite dismayed by what I saw, and even more perplexed at how this could happen. I asked the same question of the east hill blowout. Both locations were deficient in all respects, and rain readily eroded the clay away, as the runnels in the ground indicated. I realized that soil was a living entity, and that what I was looking at was a substrate almost entirely devoid of life. I had to come up with a way to bring the soils of life back to these areas. Using my limited knowledge, I decided to plant several black locusts in a random pattern on the south hill because they have the ability to fix nitrogen, and they can grow on severely compromised soils. On one edge of the south hill, the soil was too wet for black locust and I planted gray birch, which are pioneering trees able to tolerate wetland. That was it. The former owner mowed most of the landscape and now all mowing ceased on the east hill blowout and the south hill. I marveled at the transformations that took place over the next ten years from this simple start.

I was troubled by the chaotic stands of box elders in the vicinity of the creek. They were clearly not healthy. These are tough trees, but they were suffering greatly in the waterlogged soils. They were falling over in slow motion or sometimes suddenly. The extreme angles that these trees adopted, many of them horizontal, effectively screened out the light over large tracts of the landscape. Many more trees and plants could occupy the landscape if there was less shade. A single horizontal tree shaded a footprint capable of supporting thirty-five vertical trees. I felt quite bad about cutting down around a hundred fifty living box elder trees. I realized they would ultimately fall over completely and resigned myself to the fact that killing some of the existing life was necessary to improve the whole. I had not yet learned of communicating with the trees to explain the reasons for my actions. But I think they understood the sorrow I felt in my heart as I cleared the troubled trees from the land. I left the healthy box elders, some of which succumbed in time for the same reason.

I discovered that the stumps sucker readily and that cutting down the trees was only a partial solution. I had to stop the suckers, which would increase the number of trunks tenfold if left to grow, and the problem I attempted to solve would be worse than when I started. In my reading I learned that preventing light from reaching the stumps would ultimately kill the tree. The suckers seek out light, and if they do not find light, they will drain all the energy reserves in the roots, killing the tree. I had a way of solving this problem without using chemicals. I covered every stump with vegetable cans, rubber troughs used to feed pigs, black plastic sheeting, metal bushel baskets and pails depending on the diameter of the trunk. I learned that the amount of time that the stumps needed to be covered was variable. It might be one year to several years. I would check the status of the stumps every spring, and if one was decaying, I removed the cover. If not, I put the cover back on and waited another year.

I used this same technique on invasives such as buckthorn. When I attempted to pull out a buckthorn with a trunk the diameter of a pencil, I was stunned at how hard it was to even get it to budge, and even more surprised when a two-foot-diameter root ball came out with it. This definitely was making the situation worse. The buckthorn root system is an extensive fibrous mesh. I changed my approach and cut all invasive or overpopulated trees off between two and three inches above the ground, and covered them to block the light.

I was looking at the ash trees and thought they looked a bit anemic, actually very anemic, and withered. I thought perhaps some disease had hit the trees. I researched the books and could not find anything that matched my observations. I gave it some more scrutiny, because I was really concerned now since the trees were looking worse despite the ample rains. They appeared as if they were drying out. For some reason that I cannot explain, I had the thought that I should dig out the soil from the base of one of the trees. When I reached a level about four inches below the surface, I came upon some kind of wire and, with further digging, discovered it was the ID tag for the tree. The person who had planted the trees never took them off, and they were strangling the tree. I was so happy that I had found out what was wrong with them and proceeded to dig out the base of every tree that looked withered. All of them were being strangled by the ID tags. I cut them free, and all the trees rebounded at an astonishing rate.

In 1993, I became aware of a plant-hardiness rating put out by the USDA. This five-acre parcel in 1993 was climate zone 3B/4A. All of my research with field guides made it abundantly clear that plants would not survive outside their described zones or would struggle mightily. I had only my physical skill sets at this time, and the zone hardiness was central to my planting decisions. I was looking at the boglands, and these flooded extensively in the spring. My research revealed that tamarack trees thrived in bogs, but I was not very enamored with the looks of the tree. They look rather harsh in the winter, which is long here. This land was at the southern end of their survival range, and they do not tolerate the heat. Yet I felt that this was the right choice to rectify the hydrology issue in this section of the landscape. I was still only using the physical at this time. In 1995, I planted five hundred one-foot-tall tamarack trees in a random pattern through the center of a two-inch-by-two-inch square of landscape fabric to cut down on surrounding competition, and to help locate them in the sea of grass. I thought all was good, feeling very satisfied with the result. By the end of July, I realized things had gone horribly wrong, because I could not find any of the trees. I went into the bog, and the grass was about five feet tall. I searched for the trees, and to my horror, every tree I found was dead. The grass had started growing in late May, and by mid-June, it was already two feet tall. It continued to grow for another month, at which point it was between four feet and six feet tall. What happened was the grass had grown straight upward, easily outgrowing the infant trees. This cut back the amount of light reaching the trees, but the worst was yet to come. In the middle of July, the grass packed together and lay over, trapping the trees between the stalks. It completely smothered the young trees, starving them of all light, and the trees died. All five hundred trees succumbed in 1995. I replanted two hundred one-foot-tall tamaracks in 1996 and scythed the land monthly for the duration of the growing season. I chose the scythe because I could surgically remove the growing grass without harming the trees. I continued scything the ground once a month over a period of five years, until the trees were two feet taller than the tallest grass.

I was now making a transition from a fully physical approach to one that was a blend of both the physical and the spiritual. I still leaned heavily toward the physical, but there were glimmers of the spiritual in the works. My research revealed that planting small trees was better than planting large-balled and burlap-wrapped trees. A small tree is between an inch and two feet tall when planted. Before I understood how trees grew, I thought it would be better to plant big trees because they would become a big tree quicker. That is not the case. The root system is out of scale with the trunk and branches on a balled and burlap-wrapped tree. Roots grow about eighteen inches in length per year and need to come into balance with the height of the tree. The tree will not grow any taller until the roots catch up. What this means is that after seven years, the tree that was one foot tall when planted will be the same height as the tree that was eight feet tall when planted. It is much easier to plant two hundred small trees than two hundred eight-foot-tall trees and less expensive.

I had now attended several classes at the Tracker School, and I was using more and more spiritual tools. I came to realize that the barren landscape had no grandparent or parent trees to watch over and protect the infant trees and plants. As an Earth steward, I needed to function as both a parent and a grandparent until the trees became parents and could take over. In the absence of grandparents and parents, weather systems, humans and other animals had killed off the infant trees and plants before they had a chance to grow. The dominant animal problems were deer, mice, raccoons, groundhogs and rabbits. Deer eat almost all plants, and they rake the bark off trees in the fall with their antlers. Oftentimes the antler scrapes killed the tree because they were completely girdled. In the winter the mice and rabbits stripped the bark from trees, again completely girdling them. Mice also do this throughout the year with small twig-size trees. Raccoons are strong and will pull entire branches off fruiting trees. The best defense is a physical barrier, a cage surrounding the tree. This defends the tree from deer, but they are still susceptible to mice, rabbits and groundhogs. In the winter the snow can get deep enough that the rabbits and deer go over the top of the cage and eat the foliage, buds and bark depending on the species of tree. The height of the cage must take into account the depth of the winter snows. Mice and voles are small enough to get through all cages, except fine-mesh window screen. Plastic tubes will protect trees from mice, rabbits and deer. Five-foot-tall growing tubes are not tall enough to prevent deer from eating the apical meristem, the main growth leader of a tree, but they will protect the tree from antler rubs. Any fruiting tree does not do well in a grow tube: nut trees, apples, pears, peaches, cherries, apricots, pawpaws, etc. They do not work on conifers either. For these trees wire cages are necessary, held down by T posts. Deer and raccoons are strong enough to tear cages off rebar-type rods or bend them over. Groundhogs will dig under cages to eat young trees. If this is a possibility, the wire mesh needs to flare out from the base two feet beyond the cage, even with the ground. This still does not guarantee that the groundhog will not tunnel under the extended base. Defeating mice from eating bark can be accomplished by painting tree rosin or the sap or pitch of evergreens on the trunks of deciduous trees. This is most easily accomplished by dissolving it in denatured alcohol and painting it on with a paintbrush you never intend to use again. This is a diligent practice that must be done in the planting of all trees, herbaceous plants and forbs on barren, denuded ground.

These animals were not maliciously damaging the landscape, but living according to the laws of nature. The animals are extremely important allies. As an Earth steward I guided the activities of the animals toward the healing of the land. I let all the digging animals live their way: the moles, the groundhogs, the worms and the ants. They leave their marks on the landscape in the form of mounds and ridges, but they were aerating the compacted soils, eating the grubs and bringing deep nutrients back to the surface. I enlisted the birds to eat the insect pests, and provided homes for them before the shrubs and small trees became established. I favored the bald-faced hornets, paper wasps and yellow jackets because they are voracious consumers of caterpillars, beetles and flies. They also defended the land from physical invaders. I set out woodpiles for my winter fires in places where snakes could find sanctuary, because they eat mice and a wide variety of insects. I let the skunks rummage through the yard, so they would look for all manner of grubs, while loosening up the compacted soils. I smiled as I walked through the landscape, marveling at the work my animal allies were doing. They truly were important participants in the healing of the land.

As I watched over the land, one of the most frustrating aspects was the impact that humans were inflicting on the recovering land. Garbage appeared on a regular basis: all manner of bottles, plastic bags, fast-food sacks, five-gallon pails of unidentified liquids, tires with rims, furniture and the like. If I did not get these things picked up right away, the accumulation would escalate. A part of me resented the continuous policing of the landscape, but it was absolutely necessary. That was just part of the impact, for many people mindlessly throw things out, and some found it economically convenient to leave it on my landscape. There were others who inflicted more serious damage to the landscape. During the spring, the owners of mudding trucks enjoyed driving through the recently thawed-out ground, even though it was not their land. The same was true in the winter with the snowmobilers. Infant trees were invisible to both groups of individuals. They lay beneath the blanket of snow in the winter, and blended into the landscape in the early spring. I put up T posts at every tree I planted to make it obvious that this area should not be driven over. Some T posts were still driven over. No-trespassing signs also helped. In the long view, I planted trees that grew fast to block entry. Intermixed within them, I planted more substantial trees. When the fast trees ultimately died or broke in storms, the robust trees would be in place.

I relied on my guardian plants to protect the land during the growing season. These arrived of their own accord where they were needed: the thistles, the nettles and poison ivy. Because I was an Earth steward, these guardians let me pass without causing me any discomfort or harm. However, an individual with malicious intent suffered from their wrath. They were plentiful in the early phases of the recovery, but faded away as the land returned to health. I have the utmost respect for these plants and loved walking among them.

As I gained an ever-deeper understanding of the role of the Earth steward, I came to understand the vital importance of listening to the voices of the landscape denizens, the voice of the Spirit That Moves

In and Through All Things and the voices of the Unseen and Eternal. I found it was possible to communicate with a plant and ask it where it wished to be planted. I would ask a question of a particular region, "What trees should be growing here?" I would place an order for the trees as directed, but each plant or tree was a unique individual, the same as people. Some liked more heat. Some liked more cold. Some needed more water, less light and more shelter. In the case of trees, once they arrived, it was a long process of planting them. I would pick up the tree or plant and ask, "Where would you like to be planted?" Sometimes the answer was quick and definitive. It knew exactly where it wanted to be planted. In other cases, it was unsure, and I walked the landscape with this plant, asking whether it liked a particular spot or not. Oftentimes it still did not know where it wanted to live. So I brought it back and repeated the process the next day. Eventually, it decided where it wanted to live, and I planted it there.

I also became aware that many trees were in trouble in the wild places, and there was talk of shifts in the climate. I have a strong attachment to trees and wanted to preserve as many species as I could. I felt directed to provide sanctuary for many tree species that are at risk and struggling in the wild. An example is the butternut tree, afflicted by a blight that decimated their ranks in the wild. Other rare trees include the yellowwood and the dawn redwood. Some of these trees are vulnerable to climate change because they cannot migrate fast enough. At the start of my restoration, the climate was zone 3B/4A. In twenty years, it shifted a half zone to 4A/4B. When I started planting zone 5 trees twenty years ago, I did my utmost to listen to the voice of the plant and planted many species of zone 5 trees in the zone 3B/4A climate, some individuals died, but many survived. Eight species of zone 5 trees are still living after fifteen to twenty years in this zone 3B/4A/4B climate. Currently there are fourteen species of zone

5 trees living on this land. Over the past twenty years, the climate has warmed 5 degrees Fahrenheit, and the process of planting became much easier for me. I am very fond of these trees, and I monitored them more closely than the native trees. It will not be long before the climate shifts to 5B, and these trees will be in their element.

This poses another problem for the extraordinarily cold-hardy tamarack trees, planted to manage the flooding, where their southern survival limit is zone 4. They will struggle when the climate shifts to zone 5. I was not using the spiritual skills when I planted these trees, but as time moved forward and I assessed where they live, I determined that there is a bit of an extended window for them. They are sited where the microclimate remains cold and cool relative to the surrounding landscape. This region of the landscape should function as a zone 4 region when the surrounding landscape shifts to zone 5 for a period of time.

The landscape had several invasives that needed management or eradication: buckthorn, wild cucumber, wild grape, Virginia creeper and spotted knapweed. Buckthorn was planted by birds, so every year there were new trunks to cut off and cover with a can. Wild cucumbers, wild grapes, and Virginia creeper grew so extensively that they completely engulfed the young or even substantial trees. They either smothered it to death or distorted the growth habit of the tree, bending the leader off at a bizarre angle. These vines were cut off at ground level and pulled out of the trees. I searched out the young growth in early spring so I could remove them before vines developed, since it was much less work than pulling the vines out of trees.

Spotted knapweed is native to Europe and it has invaded approximately seven million acres in North America.[1] It is very successful because it is unpalatable to herbivores and has a taproot that pulls in water more readily than neighboring plants. It also produces catechin, a phytotoxin it exudes from its roots that stunts the growth of adjacent plants. The way I controlled this was to wait until after a heavy rainstorm softened the soil, and then I pulled as many out by hand as time allowed. I wore gloves when pulling knapweed because it contains carcinogens.[1, 2, 3] If the entire root is not pulled out, it regrows, which is why I waited until after a substantial rain softened the soil. There was seed stock in the soil, but with diligent weeding, they ultimately expired. Pulling was very effective because it resulted in minimal disturbance of the surrounding ground, and the land where the knapweed formerly grew rebounded to full health within two weeks of pulling the weed. It took two years to pull all the existing knapweed out, followed by another three years of pulling any new ones before they went to seed. After that period of time, there might be one or two plants at most per year.

As time moved forward, the black locusts rebuilt the soil on the south hill. New herbaceous plants moved in of their own accord. I added an additional forty-eight species of herbaceous plants to the landscape to balance things out. Animal life increased, birds moved in and built nests in the small trees and the stinging insects built homes throughout the landscape, in trees and on structures. I continually added more tree species as the health of the land recovered. The recovery was very slow at first. The black locusts did not grow much for the first five years, many of them died and some were taken out by locust borers. The soil relationship with the roots took time to develop. Twenty-three years later, the hill is lush with all manner of plants, grasses, forbs and trees. I love going onto that hill and looking at what once was cracked, dried ground and experiencing awe at the transformation.

The once scraggly white spruce in the yard recovered as fertilizers and herbicides leached from the land. It is now vibrant with life. The trees girdled by the nursery labels are full, strong trees. The blowout on the east hill smoothed out on its own and is filled with all manner of wild herbaceous plants. No spray was ever applied to the fruit trees. The birds and stinging insects keep the harmful insects in check. The moles tunnel through the grass, eating the grubs, and the gophers build their mounds. The ants build enormous complexes in the forest and do a marvelous job of reducing the canned trunks to soil. The yard has never been watered. It is filled with clover, dandelions, heal-all, plantain, pussytoes, oxeye daisy's, yarrow, clover and wood sorrel. It is green in all seasons and changes its green hue practically every week. There is something in bloom from April until November, providing food for the pollinators, which are abundant throughout the year. What was once a scraggly, withered landscape is now lush in all seasons.

In May of 2016, I was walking through the yard, taking note of tracks and plant life, when I spotted a plant I have never seen before. It was an innocuous, short plant that blended into the grass so well that I almost missed it. I was so captivated by this plant that I found a large stick and stuck it in the ground so I could find it again. I was extremely excited about this find, for this was a truly exotic plant. This was a very unusual occurrence. I had to figure out what this plant was. I knew what it was not, which greatly shortened the hunt for the identity of this mystery plant, and I love solving mysteries. Within a day, I had identified the plant as a twayblade orchid. What is so significant about this plant?

What I learned was that the twayblade orchid is protected by the federal Species at Risk Act (SARA).[4] This is an orchid that has a symbiotic relationship with a specific soil fungus, a particular strain of mycorrhizal fungus, the Rhizoctonia/Tulasnella fungus.[5,6] If that fungus is not present it will not grow. Mycorrhizae fungi are delicate and are easily damaged or killed by tilling the soil, by pesticides and by fertilizers.[7, 8] Residential lawns are grossly overfertilized; in addition, they are subject to all manner of herbicides and pesticides. These residues remain in the soil and retard the growth or destroy the mycorrhizae. These fungi are a critical element in the health of plants because they form a symbiotic relationship with the root structure. The surface area of the mycorrhizae is many hundreds of times larger than that of the plant to which it is coupled. Lacking this fungus, the plants suffer from fewer nutrients and less water. The first indicator of the disappearing chemical load was the rebound of the white spruce. But it was not until the twayblade arrived that I could say that the soil had recovered. It took twenty-four years from the termination of the chemical assault. It reminded me of the spiritual communication that came to me seventeen years ago explaining that I would need patience. At that time I'd had no idea what that message really meant, but now the meaning of patience is much clearer.

At the beginning of my Earth stewardship efforts twenty-three years ago, there were thirty-five species of trees that inhabited the land, of which five no longer exist: two because they succumbed to disease, and the remaining three were removed because of their invasive characteristics. Over that time an additional 175 species of trees were planted, of which forty-seven ultimately succumbed. Now an additional 128 species of trees live on the land, bringing the total number of different tree species to 159. All told 2,172 trees were planted. Many trees were purchased, but a significant number were started from seeds acquired from catalogs or by collecting them from sidewalks, paths, roads or trees. In a wild forest each tree you see standing is the final survivor of eight thousand seedlings; 7,999 trees succumbed to some force of nature. Because I am an Earth steward, it is possible to surpass this survival rate by an enormous margin. Mankind has disturbed all places of the Earth in some way, some more than others. When we have the mind-set of an Earth steward, more of the Earth can be brought back to health and balance. Anyone can make the choice to take this journey.

Philip Martin, PhD

ENDNOTES

1. https://en.wikipedia.org/wiki/Centaurea_maculosa

2. http://www.dnr.state.mn.us/invasives/terrestrialplants/herbaceous/spottedknapweed.html

3. https://catalog.extension.oregonstate.edu/sites/catalog/files/project/pdf/ec1596.pdf

4. https://wildlife-species.canada.ca/species-risk-registry/species/speciesDetails_e.cfm?sid=227

5. http://www.illinoiswildflowers.info/savanna/plants/pp_twayblade.htm

6. http://www.newfs.org/docs/pdf/Liparis%20liliifolia.pdf

7. http://www.luvnpeas.org/edibility/edibleFiles/mycorrhizae.html

8. http://www.esf.edu/melnhe/News/Megan%20McLin.pdf